THE POWER OF WHY 29 MUSICIANS CLIMBED TO SUPERSTAR

GLORY ST. GERMAIN

GLORYLAND PUBLISHING

COPYRIGHT

Copyright © 2021 by Gloryland Publishing Glory St. Germain.

All rights reserved. The rights of Gloryland Publishing to be identified as the publisher of the compilation have been asserted by them in accordance with the Copyright Act of Canada.

This book has been co-authored by 29 writers. Copyright for each chapter belongs to the individual author. The greatest care has been taken in compiling this book. However, no responsibility is accepted by the publishers or compilers for the accuracy of the information presented in this book.

Where opinion is expressed it is that of the author of individual chapters and does not necessarily coincide with that of the publisher of this book.

No part of this book may be reproduced or transmitted in any form or by any means, electronic or mechanical, including photocopying, recording, or by any information storage and retrieval system, without prior permission in writing from the publisher.

For any inquiries or permissions, contact the publisher.

info@UltimateMusicTheory.com

Compiled By: Glory St. Germain

Edited By: Wendy H. Jones and Lisa McGrath

Cover Design By: Glory St. Germain

DEDICATION

To my grandparents and parents who surrounded me with the joy of learning music and inspired me to reach for the stars. If you believe with all your heart, then you can achieve anything.

To my Superstar husband Ray, for sharing your legendary voice with the world and always shining your light so bright. To our children and grandchildren for being the twinkling stars that light up my life. Thank you.

I love you all.

CONTENTS

1. From Self to Service — 1
2. How do you get to Carnegie Hall? Practice, Practice, Practice. — 6
3. Quest for Your Authentic Self — 10
4. Enriching the World with the Gift of Music, One Person at a Time — 14
5. Against All Odds — 18
6. Music, Feeling, and Dance — 22
7. The Superstar Game — 26
8. If The Shoe Fits, Wear It — 31
9. The Crooked Path to Owning The Stage — 37
10. The Rise to Superstar — 42
11. Keep Going — 47
12. Piano Teaching - Spreading Joy and Passion — 51
13. Music was a Calling that Led the Way — 55
14. Creating Superstar Students — 59
15. Music as Connection — 64
16. Entrepreneurial Resilience — 69
17. Super-Star Creator — 73
18. Success is Your Story — 78
19. A Long, Slow Ascent to Superstardom — 82
20. Reach For the Stars, But Remember Who You Are — 87
21. Highs and Lows and Highs — 91
22. My Grandma's Dying Wish — 96
23. What It Takes to Live a Meaningful Life — 100
24. Adventure in Dreamland from East to West — 104
25. The Heart Journey to The Star — 109
26. Notes from Miss Mac — 114
27. A Musical Journey From Japan to Berklee — 118
28. After a Lifetime — 122
29. The Climb to Reach the Stars — 126

About the Author 131
Acknowledgments 133
Afterword – The Magic of Wishing on a Star 135
Also by Glory St. Germain 137

1

FROM SELF TO SERVICE

Randall Faber
USA

Age twenty-one...small rumblings in my mind. Conflicted. I relished the teenage glory of winning competitions, recording contracts, radio play, and photos in the newspaper. But my religious Midwest upbringing urged humility. What's going on with my ego?

Am I a gentle spirit or this kick-butt pianist with long hair? My arrogant self and my humble self wouldn't have the conversation. Yet, I knew each intimately. I let this schizophrenia remain unresolved because, at this time of life, I needed to focus on the power of dominating my instrument. It was an intuition. It was me. I was driven. Practice, practice, practice!

I was an unlikely musician. In fourth grade I saw a folder on my classmate's desk. Emblazoned on the cover was the word *Choir*. What's that word? I presumed a misspelling of chore. Perhaps a task list? Must not be important. Maybe I was too good to be assigned "chores"? In scanning the room, it became clear that everyone had this folder, except me...and my six-foot buddy who was already sprouting a moustache. I found out at the Christmas concert that we were the only students not allowed to sing in the choir. And this was a required class! I didn't mind. My voice was too low to sing, I figured. And I was very much engaged with the stack of LP (long-playing) records that the music teacher had given me at the end of the last school year. Must have been a consolation prize.

I learned the value of practice early on. My older brother played first-chair trumpet. He taught me when I was six. So, when I entered school band in the 5th grade, I had a solid head start...a few years of piano lessons plus years on my horn. Boring, I thought. I lazily lorded over the cornet section from my seat as 1st chair. The early challenges went fine, but I was unmotivated—even unwilling–to practice these easy exercises. I didn't want my mother or brother to hear me on such an elementary repertoire. The end-of-year challenges taught me something important. I had not practiced, but everyone else had. The first challenger outplayed me, and I dropped to second chair. Realizing the opportunity and my lack of preparation, everyone went after me. I felt like a duck being hunted by a pack of wolves. I dropped to 5th, then 6th, then 7th chair. Humiliated. That won't happen again, I said convincingly to myself. I quit band.

It is easy to define the What of success. And the How is clear, at least in retrospect: single-minded focus plus a wide-lens perspective. Long hours of hard work...much more than your peers. Disciplined routines. A lot of risk, and a bit of luck. For "preparation to meet opportunity" it helps to know the right people at the right time. This means being adventurous enough to put your foot in the door.

But Why? That is a deeper question. Why the drive to succeed? Why the commitment to long hours, to excellence?

One might guess talent. I didn't have musical talent but was very smart. I worked hard and developed musical talent. The interesting point is that when I was playing really well, when people said, "Isn't he talented!" I felt the obligation to work even harder. I felt that gifts were from God, and our obligation is to maximize these gifts. So, talent develops, it is earned. And the more it develops the greater the obligation to work hard to develop further.

This thinking sounds circular, but it illustrates two points.

1) Talent is not merely genetic; it emerges through environmental engagement. The more one learns and practices, the greater the talent. And the greater the talent, the more supportive opportunities arise for greater development. This is not talent plus environment; it is a series of transactional, mutual influences between talent and environment.

2) If one adheres to the belief that talents are gifts to be cultivated, then successes lead to more successes. This could be called the self-enhancement hypothesis. We're drawn to what we're good at.

I've learned that we repeat what we repeat. We do more of what we do. Part of this is physiology—neural development. What we do repetitively eventually generates a highway of neural connectivity. It is easy to do what we do again and again. So, skill brings more skill.

From a psychological standpoint, we grow up needing to demonstrate our effectiveness in the world. We crave competence. We appreciate talent, especially our own. As we age into the teen years, the need is identity. An area of talent fills this need beautifully. Yes, another motivational layer. We do more of what feeds our identity.

Is this why, when others at music school went to the cafeteria to socialize, I was in the practice room catching a few more minutes on my trills and octaves? Why for many years I sought out a Steinway Grand in the classroom and practiced until 1 AM, when the janitor would boot me out night after night? The inherent need to demonstrate competence and to embrace an identity offer compelling answers.

Yet, I don't think this is the full story. Many musicians work hard. Many have developed enormous talent. Yet not all have the experience of career and good fortune.

I believe the above describes the Why of preparation. Why we begin and engage in disciplined commitment. But success is not just about oneself. It starts there but transforms "from self to service." When a wider perspective allows you to transcend ego, you'll find that a career derives from what you can give, not what you take. Taking scholarships and applause is only preparation. A career begins when you add value for others.

This is the real Why. It launched a rocket trajectory for me. I'm grateful for the Roland Lifetime Achievement Award in Education, the Keyboard Pedagogy Award from the Music Teacher National Association and Frances Clark Center, and the Distinguished Service Award as a Steinway Artist. Note that these appear as personal validations but are really acknowledgments of contribution. Presenting the keynote address in Beijing for China Reading Day was an honor bestowed because of the value delivered through hundreds of previous lectures and workshops. Nancy and I sell millions of books around the world because the books provide real value for others.

"From self to service" resolved my ego vs. humility dilemma. It brought together myself and Nancy as a power duo. It rallied and coalesced our support team. And, as a wonderful bonus, skill plus service go hand-in-hand with happiness and peace of mind.

How might you apply your unique talents in service of others?

Author Bio:

Randall Faber, PhD, is co-author of the bestselling Piano Adventures® method, published in 10 languages. He lectures and performs at major universities and conferences around the world.

https://PianoAdventures.com

2

HOW DO YOU GET TO CARNEGIE HALL? PRACTICE, PRACTICE, PRACTICE.

Rami Bar-Niv
Israel/USA

Being asked to contribute a chapter to this book took me by surprise. I don't know about being a superstar, but I do know about climbing. Climbing means to me continuous, sincere hard work, despite many obstacles and personal tragedies. An adult student and friend who read my autobiography remarked, "You did well for the first seventy-five years of your life..." Give me another seventy-five years and maybe I will climb to superstar.

When I was seven years old, I read a children's book about Mozart, and I cried because I wanted to be like him. A few years ago, an orchestra premiered my Israeli Suite and my youngest grandchild, who was in the audience, witnessed the conductor inviting me to take a bow after the orchestra performed my piece. He then asked me, "Are you famous, Grandpa?" My mother was my first piano teacher and lived her life for me and my music career. For years, whenever I returned home from a concert tour abroad, I went to see my mother and had to show her the various newspaper clippings and reviews of the concerts. Then she would say, "So, you are famous now."

In 1985, I performed at the home of the Vered family. Thirty years later, I met Mr. Vered at the swimming pool. We didn't recognize each other, and he asked for my name. When I replied, "Rami Bar-Niv" he said, "Get out of here, you are not Rami Bar-Niv, Rami Bar-Niv is a famous pianist who performed at my home thirty years ago." All over the world people approached me after my concerts telling me that they had heard me before in other countries. People told me that they have had my record albums for years. People could not believe that I lived in Israel; they thought that an international artist had to live abroad. Pianists told me that I was their idol when they were children, and conductors told me they grew up listening to my records. Someone recently told me that I was a living legend. I never realized I was, nor did I consider myself to be, famous. I just did my work and the rest, it seems, took care of itself. I had millions of 'listens' on MP3.com in the early days of the Internet. I toured and gave concerts all over the world. It felt good when on my tours I kept on running into the big-name artists being on the same concert series as I was. It was exciting to perform in beautiful concert halls that had a back-stage gallery with photos of famous artists like Rubinstein, Arau, and others who had performed there. What a feeling of exaltation it was to perform on the same stages and play on the same pianos that these legends did. It felt quite grand performing for 3000 people in Boston and for 5000 people in Mexico City. It did feel great to perform in Carnegie Hall, in Lincoln Center, in the iconic old Town Hall in NYC, in the concert hall inside the Forbidden City in Beijing, in magnificent concert halls in South America, Europe, and the rest of the world. It was an honor and a pleasure to perform for, have in my audience, and share the stage with, Isaac Stern, Jan Peerce, Henny Youngman, Sidney Poitier, Paul Paray, Lukas Foss, Leonard Bernstein, Artur Rubinstein, Leopold Godowsky III (Gershwin's nephew), Leonid Hambro, and many other artists of stature.

It was exciting when the sheet music of my compositions started selling in music stores and on Internet sites; students, pianists, instrumentalists, and orchestras started performing and recording my pieces, and my name appeared on concert programs along with the great composers. When my piano-fingering book started selling like hot potatoes, I knew I contributed something important to the world of pianism and for future generations. When my students thanked me and called me "Rami Bar-None," I was moved for reaching their hearts and for the impact my teaching had on them.

As international newspapers, magazines, radio, and TV programs kept on asking me for interviews, my photos started appearing in the media alongside big names. Radio, TV, and Internet podcasts kept on playing my recordings, so I felt I was continuing to climb. Fellow musicians, actors, and artists asked to perform with me, which made me feel accepted by the artist community.

In 1982, I made history by being the first and only Israeli artist to ever perform in Egypt following the Begin/Sadat Peace Treaty, when in 1989 I received the best performer award from the Israeli government, and when in 2012 someone opened a Wikipedia page about me, I realized I was still climbing.

Music and piano playing aren't just my passion, they are my life! I didn't plan it that way, but my children were born when I was performing on the stage. Tragedies happened to me and my family when I was far away on concert tours. My music career was demanding but nothing would stand in the way of passion-driven determination. New stars appeared and disappeared. My own concert career was never meteoric. It was just a slow, steady, and stubborn climb. I didn't compare myself to others; just did my own thing. My karate teacher taught me, "You are your own greatest opponent." That meant to me - compete only with myself, not with others.considering my six decades of world-wide concert tours, my recordings, LP albums with Columbia Records and other labels, audio cassettes, CDs, video cassettes, DVDs, and YouTube videos, considering my published and performed compositions, my published books, and my thousands of posts in various groups on the Internet, I know I have created and will be leaving behind some legacy.

Before I end this chapter of mine, I'll share this little story. In one of my concerts at the Vermont piano camp for adults where I was teaching for ten years, the admiring campers prepared a surprise for me. After I played the first piece of my program, they suddenly turned off the lights, lit lighters they had bought in town earlier during the day and waved them with their hands up in the air, like it's done with candles in rock concerts. That made me feel like I was a rock superstar. But more importantly, it made me feel loved and appreciated.So, I say to you all - perseverance! Believe in yourself, be serious about what you're doing, study hard, do your own thing and do not look sideways, compete only with yourself, fight only yourself, and better yourself.

Author Bio:

Rami Bar-Niv, international pianist, composer, author, teacher. Born: Tel-Aviv, 1945. Graduated: Rubin Academy of Music, NYC's Mannes College of Music. Founded "Rami's Rhapsody Piano Camp". Authored "The Art of Piano fingering", "Blood, Sweat, and Tours".

http://www.ybarniv.com/rami

3

QUEST FOR YOUR AUTHENTIC SELF

Matt Becks
USA

I never chose music, music chose me. My dad, a great singer/songwriter, and my mom, teacher and excellent piano player and singer, put me in a special music program in a private music school when I was this six-year-old Tasmanian devil tornado. I became familiar with different instruments, having theory and singing lessons but also switching back-and-forth between piano and violin for one year before having to decide which one of those two I'd be studying intensively. I loved the piano so much.

I quickly felt the need to create music. I sometimes got in trouble because I was at my piano improvising and creating instead of practicing. The authorities, who I occasionally had a little problem with, got tired of my comedic skills and kicked me out in 6th grade. Going from elementary to high school, I joined an Air Force program and discovered brass. I then studied the trombone, as well as theory and singing for five years. I'm not sure why I chose the trombone because I was still so attracted and fascinated by the drums. Well, one of the reasons why was actually a mistake by my teachers, as they wouldn't let me spend my energy on drums saying I was too disturbing. How paradoxical. Either when I was supposed to practice trombone in school or the military, I'd put it aside to go jam on drums and percussion, getting in trouble from time to time. I couldn't resist. Some older folks recognized and appreciated my talent. One of my first bands was a tribute to Led Zeppelin.

What an amazing school. I learned to play drums, listened, and study John Bonham. I became popular pretty quickly performing a Moby Dick drum solo and next thing you know, I was part of half of the bands in high school, writing original music already. It's when I was seventeen that the notorious jazz drummer and teacher Mr. Masson saw me play Sunday morning at church and said, "You're coming to study drums with me at Lionel-Groulx." I said yes pretty much immediately. To be honest, I was the most undisciplined student you'd ever seen. All I wanted to do was play and have fun. Little did I know that playing drums would very soon put bread on the table.

I joined the original band Redcore, and we recorded an album as I was finishing college. I was playing a gig in a biker club every Wednesday when they approached me. Our electrifying performances were one of the reasons why Redcore won a big contest that got us to play festivals with Live, Moist, Foo Fighters, A Perfect Circle, Smashing Pumpkins, Sum 41, and others. Playing in front of gigantic crowds is a blast. We also got to tour Europe. Like so many other bands, it fell apart just before taking off. Back then I was also playing with Alan Gerber, a blues man from Chicago. Big contrast with Redcore's eclecticism with heavy flavors! Throughout my twenties, I got to perform at the International Montreal Jazz Festival with different artists. Opening for George Thorogood was for sure a highlight. But my ambition was not being fed. I'd been on the road of broken dreams before. I reminded myself to stay positive, keep my head straight and keep evolving - facing obstacles is inevitable. Playing all different types of music and instruments was fun. Staying on my discovery path, I ended up dancing, acting, doing voiceovers, and even comedy!

Fun fact, when working with Rene Dupéré for the Cirque Du Soleil, he didn't know I was a professional drummer and thought I was a singer and dancer. Acting, creating, and performing for the TV show Solstrom for the Cirque was such a learning experience. Staying on exploration mode got me to work on the fascinating show "Beat, La Fiesta Mondial de Percussions." This was a very interesting concept using everything except conventional percussion, like wheel caps, garbage cans, etc. Impersonating one of the Blues Brothers by dancing, singing, and being silly was delightful. Be silly, take risks, and challenge yourself. I remember the musical director (Beat) calling me for a new gig asking if I could play the didgeridoo. I said yes, but I couldn't and had to go take lessons as it was for Toyota's big annual show. Crazy.

Before leaving my hometown of Montreal, I was part of the new Bran Van 3000 band but a new project with my cousin would give me the push I needed to change my name and move to La La Land where I've been living since 2009. We ended up touring with 30 Seconds to Mars on two US tours. My blood could have hired someone local in the US but one of the reasons I got the job is because I'd kept myself up to date with hybrid drumming, incorporating electronic elements with acoustic ones, aiming to be as versatile as possible, and being able to sing at the same time was a game changer too. Arena shows with 3STM were great. Then I ended up working and co-producing this amazing Bran Van 3000 (unreleased) album for almost two years here in California.

I recorded with legendary musicians like Abraham Laboriel, Tim Pierce, Kim Bullard, and Nick Mancini. More recently in 2018, after I toured with State To State, I got a gig in Las Vegas singing and playing on the Argentina show called "Fuerza Bruta." Sadly, the main investor pulled the plug after only a couple of months. Devastating but fun for the time being. Back to Los Angeles. I met with an old friend, and fan of my old band Beatnik Jr., the mixing engineer, producer, and Grammy award winner, Gerry "The Gov" Brown. I fell in love with his music and vice versa, and we started to work together. Next thing you know, I was mixing for John Legend and ended up getting a Grammy certificate for the album *Big Love*. I never thought I would end up wearing that hat.

Here's the deal, be real, be passionate, open-minded, stay amazed, keep learning, be kind and humble, and be sure it'll lead you to awesome and memorable adventures. You're serving the art. And it's OK if you're not 100% sure where you're going with your creativity; trust the process. It's the journey that matters. Approach each performance like it was the last one: focus on musicality, telling a story. I believe those are the reasons why I got to live all those amazing experiences. Everything is possible.

Author Bio:

Matt Becks is a multi-instrumentalist, singer/songwriter, music producer, mixing engineer, actor, worked with the Cirque Du Soleil, John Legend, Chris Brown, 30 Seconds To Mars and many others.

https://www.instagram.com/mattbecks/

4

ENRICHING THE WORLD WITH THE GIFT OF MUSIC, ONE PERSON AT A TIME

Dorothy Chia
Singapore

Music gives expression to the soul and spirit of the human race. Music allows us to be human. To express joys, sorrows, fears, anger, and all the myriad of feelings that make us human. It is universal. A baby, before it learns to utter the first words, experiences a mother's heartbeat. When a baby cries, it is soothed by the singing of his mother's voice. Music is a gift that God / the greater Universe has given to humanity. How joyful it is, to be able to plant that gift of Music into every soul that I meet. I am from Singapore. I am a piano teacher, a pedagogue, an author, and a social media influencer. I am passionate about sharing my gift of music with every soul that I meet in this journey of life. I am on a mission to enrich one person at a time with the gift of music.

As a music teacher, I teach students, young and old, to play the piano. In my thirty years of molding young musicians, I have learnt that acquiring the skill of playing the piano far outweighs the Asian mentality of chasing exam certificates and competition trophies. If I am able to focus on the music, helping the young musician to play a piece of Chopin for example, beautifully, this brings me joy. To master the technical skill in order to achieve the correct intonation. To garner greater cantabile and rubato by flexing the rhythmic pulse in the music. To understand the theory behind the harmony used by Chopin in his composition and therefore, to project the intent of the composer through one's interpretation of the music. Isn't that a far superior goal to obtain than chasing after a distinction in an exam or piano competition? Life is not a race. Excellence can be reached, by patiently mastering, practicing, fixing, drilling, and sticking to the task of working through the difficult spots until it becomes easy upon mastery. Excellence is not about finishing abrsm grade 8 exam at primary 6 (twelve years old), and thereafter retiring the piano into the storeroom, never to see it again. Excellence is for every piano student to take home a skill, polish it and bloom again and again because they find joy in music long after the last piano lesson they have with me.

I am a piano pedagogue. I teach piano teachers the skill of teaching students how to play the piano. "I know how to eat doesn't mean I know how to cook," likewise, "I know how to play the piano doesn't mean I know how to teach." Teaching is a skill, likewise with piano pedagogy. I believe that every serious piano teacher should get a teaching certification. In Singapore, this could be a teaching diploma from abrsm, Trinity-Guildhall or Lcm. Mentoring young piano teachers has always been a joy for me. Many of the graduates of Forte Music Training move on to teach at major music schools or even set up their own music business after their time with me. That definitely has a compounding effect on my initial mission to enrich one person at a time with music.

I believe in the superpower of media outreach. In the 90's,

when the internet was fairly new and I was a newly minted graduate from the prestigious University of Michigan, Ann Arbor, I employed various media to reach out. My very first published book, *An Introduction to Score Reading* sold over 5,000 copies. *Theory Explorer*, a music theory book for children that I wrote back in 2014 is in its second print run. While, *Piano Pedagogy*, a workbook resource for piano teachers has been purchased by piano teachers from the United Kingdom to Australia, and from Hong Kong to Malaysia. I have also moved from my early days of blogging on social media to vlogging over YouTube. People wonder why? The naysayers around me would sniggle behind my back, thinking that I am chasing fame and power. This is what I believe in, "Real power is the dissemination of knowledge to those who seek it." Very often, at a piano lesson in my music studio, I work with only one student at a time. I am bounded by location and time. If I am very secure in my intention of enriching the world with the gift of music, one person at a time, then I am not afraid of the perception of the public. People who truly know me, know the purity of my intent and that is sufficient because I answer to no one except myself and to God.

One does not grow in solitude. The gift of music must be enriched through community. The skill of playing the piano takes talent but also hard work to master. I am happy to have started several Facebook communities where parents of budding pianists gather to share the music of their children on the piano. I am constantly finding ways that learners and teachers can grow in a community. In the era of the Covid-19 pandemic, I have witnessed how a sense of community, even in the virtual sphere, is helpful to bring people from all parts of the world together. I used to hold monthly meetups through meetup.com for piano teachers to come together. These gatherings will be informal and could be centered on a specific topic such as teaching aids, music theory, method books etc. When I teach alone, I am bound by only the ideas that I come up with. But in a community, sharing takes place and the human spirit works in a different way. When people come together to share freely, it instigates further sharing to occur. Love and kindness propagates more love and kindness. In the darkness of night, the glow from a single candle can shed powerful light for others to see.

My mission is to plant the seed of music, one person at a time.

Author Bio:

Dorothy Chia is a piano teacher, author and owner of Forte Music Training. Dorothy holds a Master of Music from the University of Michigan. She plays the piano, pipe organ, and harp.

www.fortemusictraining.com

5

AGAINST ALL ODDS

Louise Earhart
USA

I believe in Divine Intervention! This came to me during the following anecdote, which also illuminated to me that my life has allowed me to become a musician against all odds.

In a conversation with a college friend, I learned that a classmate would be directing a musical in Los Angeles. I had not stayed connected with our friend. I was not told where he would be performing in LA and, since I live in Long Beach, I dismissed it from my mind.

Later, I had some free time before I started teaching. I thought I would read something. I picked up a free Long Beach Newspaper. I read it in its entirety to the very last page. The last page announced a production in Long Beach and that the musical director was my friend. I went to the show, told the ushers that I knew the director from college, and could I see him. He came through the door with a smile, gave me a hug, and it seemed no time had passed since we were in school. It was like seeing a long-lost brother. What joy!

How does this relate to my life? It showed me that my life has been like a puzzle in which all the pieces clearly fit together. I will tell this story in three parts: formative years from childhood to college, middle years through my second and third music degree, and my career in California.

Formative Years

I was born into a privileged family as the third of three children in West Virginia. As with many children, I was drawn to music. I made up songs, poetry, and loved life. My parents built a new house. They had inherited money. Life was good. My father was wonderful to me. I was his only girl and his delight. But the clouds were darkening. He began to drink increasingly, and his work let him go. To survive, we moved to a town in Ohio where he took a position far below his intellectual level. We moved often in that same town. I went to many grade schools.

We had a square grand piano and my mother played it sometimes. I knew that we were not able to pay the rent. Our household items were sold at public auction. I was twelve. We moved, again. We rented a house that had a piano in the foyer. That piano changed my life.

I was lonely as I had no friends. On a rainy, gloomy day, I looked at the piano and thought, "I'll try that." I used the books in the piano bench to teach myself. Then my mother found a fantastic piano teacher for me. My father was always cheering me on as he was so proud. I was so happy. Then we had to move to a new town. I lost my piano and my teacher.

In the new town, I asked the art director of the museum if I could practice on the museum's piano. My parents bought me a piano. I continued teaching myself until Easter of my junior year in college when I heard a voice in my head say, "You must have a piano teacher." A teacher accepted me, and I studied with her until I graduated.

I wanted to go to the conservatory near me but my father died in a car accident in my senior year meaning I had no idea how I would pay for my education. My teacher and her husband took me to meet the professor, and he gave me a full scholarship. It paid for only one-half of the fees. Later, someone told me about a fund available to those in our county, so I applied and I received funding.

Things were looking up. But, in my first year, my mother decided to marry someone very unlike my father. My father drank too much, but he loved me, and my piano playing. I struggled to keep my grades up, but my lonely broken heart needed all my attention. In the summer between my first and second years, I decided that I would have to work so that I could graduate cum laude. One night, I decided to figure out what my grades would have to be. My grades in everything shot up, I made my goal, and graduated cum laude.

Middle Years

Following graduation, I applied to graduate schools, but nothing seemed to work out. My piano teacher said that he had gotten a notice of a school in Illinois that needed a teaching assistant for group piano. I applied and received the TA position. After graduation, I travelled with musical friends to Europe and ended up staying a year in Munich. I found a position selling musical instruments. I was my own boss and learned skills that I never had before. I wanted to go back to being a pianist and musician and went back to my college and taught. Subsequently, I taught at a university in Michigan for three years, married, moved back to Columbus, Ohio, and entered school as a PhD student in music theory. I could not give up piano, so I kept playing and studying. The highlight of my piano career at Ohio State University was that as a music theory major, I won the concerto contest and played with the orchestra. It made the theory department happy, the piano department, not so much. I also authored a dissertation that illuminated a theorist in the eighteenth century who influenced Jean Philippe Rameau. Playing with the symphony was a high point; the dissertation was a crowning point.

When I finished my degree, a colleague called and said he would like to talk. He wanted to relocate. Was I interested in buying his school? I was, and I did. I had a wonderful time running the school, learning the business, planning recitals, teaching, being an influence. During these five years, my husband's position, along with many positions in aerospace, was terminated. He ended up in another aerospace company in California, and I followed him there.

I joined the Music Teachers' Association of California, and I taught privately. I became increasingly active in the MTAC. I was elected to the state board and served as its president. In 2019, two string players from Chicago and I started a summer festival in northern Michigan. The Ensemble Festival has helped me to become a better musician against all odds.

Author Bio:

Louise Earhart has a Bachelor's and a Master's in Piano performance, a PhD in Music Theory and has taught piano and theory for over 50 years, on the college, and private level.

https://www.facebook.com/louise.earhart

6

MUSIC, FEELING, AND DANCE

Cebo Carr
USA

My name is C.E.B.O. (pronounced See-Bow). Yes, that is an acronym for Creating Energy Beyond Ordinary. This is my story of Why I started on the road to superstar status as they say. I haven't quite reached it yet but still have some years yet to try and get there.

I guess it all started when I got accepted into a magnet program for my junior high school. I was surrounded by some of the most talented individuals I would ever meet in my life, at least that is what I thought then. Young people just developing their talents for the arts. The great thing about this program was that you had to study all the arts. So, although I was selected to go to this school because of vocal and instrumental music, I also had to study dance, musical theory, and drama. It shaped me into an artist who had an appreciation for the art, not just the product artists create. This would also be the first of many tests in my life.

I had been selected to attend this program because they recognized my musical abilities, but they had no idea about my dance abilities. I won my first dance competition at six years old, so I never even thought about dancing, it was just something I could always do. It was what I saw growing up in the Caribbean. Moving to the United States it continued into what I saw on arriving at my grandmother's apartment in the south Bronx - this new thing later called Hip Hop. I knew it at the time as just breaking and rap music. So now here I am in Irvington, New Jersey, and the musical director asks if I had danced before. Of course, I said, "Yes!" and proceeded to demonstrate some of the illest top rock and floor work. The director stopped me and said, "I don't know what that was but don't ever do that here again." Every time I tell that story people are flabbergasted but it wasn't a shock to me. No one at that time understood what we were doing, and most couldn't see or appreciate the artistry. So, I just let it go because around my neighborhood I was known as shorty that gets busy. That was enough for me.

I continued to practice at home perfecting every step I saw from anywhere I could see it. Most of it came from television. One of the biggest dancers of that time was Michael Jackson. That is where my path to superstar status began. Most people at that time were trying to dance like Michael. I, on the other hand, wanted to battle him because I knew in my soul I could dance better than him. So, I would practice day and night just in case he would be driving down my block and his car would break down and I would have a chance to battle him. That never happened, but it gave me a work ethic for practice that few street and club dancers had at that time. We were all just freestylers, but I practiced to get moves on both sides and to be able to do things at will, not just in certain situations. So, now I had the drive and the ethic I just needed one more thing: style. I would stumble upon that in high school.

Then when I hit high school, I was introduced to the underground New York City nightclub scene. If Michael was the door on the path to superstar status, The New York City underground nightclub scene was my first step through that door, and what huge first steps they were. I never saw so many people dancing how I danced. But better, way, way, way, better. I knew from that moment there was a lot I needed to learn, and for the next four years, it was school, work, and then club. Rinse and repeat.

I did not know then how things would come full circle. While everyone was paying attention to Michael, I was watching everything and everyone else in the videos and that is when I realized these dancers at the club were the dancers in just about all the videos I had watched and studied. I wanted to be known as the best, and to do that, you have to be around the best. That however was easier said than done. Being around the best in any field requires you to be at a certain level of understanding and to do that you have to be willing to be less than, so you can learn to be more than. I thought I knew everything, which made it difficult for me to learn anything. When you grow up hearing you won't make it, nothing that you do is any good and the things that have saved you are of no value to anyone. You only trust yourself and what you know. So, finding that style wasn't easy at all. I was confused!

Why I started on the road to superstar status wasn't clear at first for me. For people to value what I do, I need to know why I value what I do. Which for me meant getting to know who I was, where I came from, and why I do what I do. It was a tough road because it meant emptying my cup yet again and instead of this time just filling it up understanding the pieces I had in my cup, why I had them in my cup, and if I wanted to put them back in the cup. The path to superstardom in the street and club dance world and community means a firm understanding of who you are and what you want to contribute to the world. It also means giving thanks to the community. I am, and always have been, extremely grateful for the community and culture that has embraced me. It has given me a firm foundation to learn, teach, and support other individuals looking to find balance in their lives with music, feeling, and dance. I am still searching for the final element, and I guess once I find that maybe then I will be in that superstar status. Maybe?

Author Bio:

Terry B.J.Carr AKA Cebo is co-owner of Next Generation NYC, LLC, a member of Dance Fusion NYC. He is also artistic director of GenX The Company, rehearsal manager of Its Showtime NYC, program director for Mini X teens program, and Kinextions kids program. Spreading love through Music, Feeling, and Dance!

https://www.instagram.com/cebonxgn/

7

THE SUPERSTAR GAME

Joanne Barker
Canada

I had a plan. I was going to become a school music teacher. I was inspired by an exceptional elementary school music teacher. To me, she was a Superstar. I wanted to be just like her!

She undertook the massive task of directing a full-blown musical in her first year at the school. I was cast in the elite chorus and soon started making up my own accompaniments of the show tunes. One day, during a rehearsal break, I was at the piano playing my own version of one of the songs as my cast mates sang and danced. When the teacher and other directors entered, I thought I was in trouble. It was just the opposite. From then on, I was the fill-in rehearsal pianist.

Her school choirs won countless awards at festivals. She became known as "the" music teacher in the area - a Superstar among her peers!

During my high school years, I continued to take piano

lessons, with my goal being to study music at university. I made many trips to visit my former elementary school music teacher. At age eighteen, she invited me to become the school accompanist, a role I enjoyed for the next ten years. I was accompanist for two musicals, countless music festival performances, and school concerts. She was a very demanding choir director and shaped me as a musician.

However, my dream of teacher superstardom was not to be. At the end of my first year of university, I had extensive knee surgery which demanded months of physiotherapy. I decided to study piano to complete the Associate Degree. Unfortunately, after the completion of the Grade 10 exam, I was diagnosed with severe tendonitis. I could only play piano for about a half hour at a time. My piano lessons came to an end.

By this time, I had already established myself as a successful piano teacher and poured myself into teaching. I was constantly on the lookout for innovative ways to help students learn. I found myself scouring music stores looking for games. Store bought games were few and far between and very expensive.

After several years, I made the decision to offer group lessons. Games became even more important. I purchased books on how to make games and went to work with craft supplies to make my first creations!

Thanks to guidance from a very good friend, those early works morphed into computer designed, professionally printed and laminated items. Together, with her artistic flair and my understanding of music, a complete line of games, aids and posters were created. Without her input, I would never have been able to learn how to get my ideas from my head and into software and onto a printed page. In no time, we were selling our wares at teacher meetings and international conferences. After about ten years, our days of selling to other teachers came to an end.

I didn't think I would ever put my creative side to work again.

Then, I met Glory St. Germain at the UMTC Training Course in the summer of 2012. Soon after, she invited me to become a member of the UMT Team as Games Designer. I was so excited to be able to share my joy of creating once again!

Then life came to a stop. I was diagnosed with breast cancer. The process of surgery, chemotherapy, and radiation was quite overwhelming at times. I endured delays in treatment and was diagnosed with viral pneumonia halfway through chemo, which was really scary!

That lesson year - my "cancer" year - was really tough. I had over eighty students enrolled in group piano classes, plus several early childhood classes. My energy was so low at times. I did not feel at all creative. It was all I could do to muster up the strength to teach. I wondered if my creative energy would ever return. It took months. I needed to allow myself time to get through the treatment and heal, both mentally and physically. Glory was a very understanding, supportive, and patient friend during those long months.

Eventually, my creative juices started to flow again. I was ready to live life to the fullest and get back to designing. I was not left with "chemo brain" which I credit to two things - the fact that I am a musician and that I have a brain that functions best in "creation" mode. My first UMT games were made into game packs which teachers could purchase, already printed, laminated and ready to play.

Glory`s vision to create the Ultimate Music Theory Teachers Membership became a reality in the fall of 2020. The membership was to have monthly, themed games - in seven different levels. The task was a massive one, but one that I accepted with joy!

I find myself getting lost in the creating process. What theme should I use? What graphic will work the way I need it too? Will it serve the needs of the teacher AND the student? Is it fun? In 2020, I started creating online interactive games and activities. I have more ideas than I have hours in a day. This new virtual world has opened up endless possibilities for game creation for me.

At the start of my career, my vision was to become a Superstar School Teacher - the one students love and remember forever. That vision was not to be.

I am proud to be known as the Ultimate Music Theory Creative Design Manager. Teachers often send messages to thank me for my work and often tell me just how much their students enjoy my games. While I may not be a conventional Superstar, my games are enjoyed by teachers around the world. If being known in many countries counts - then I have definitely reached that milestone.

Achieving superstardom in anything requires a lot of effort. It also requires a vision of what you want to achieve, tools to help develop your talent and the opportunity to rise above the crowd.

I am blessed to have three people who have helped me along my journey. I am grateful to that school teacher who inspired my vision to become a Superstar. I am grateful to my good friend who taught me how to use the tools I needed to take my creations to the next level.

Lastly, I am grateful to Glory St. Germain for being the person who saw my potential and gave me the opportunity to share my creations. Without Glory, I would never have had the chance to share my love for creating with the world!

Author Bio:

Joanne Barker, UMTC Elite Educator, Piano Teacher, Composer, UMT Creative Design Manager, Author. She is the course creator of her own hybrid piano lesson system. Joanne combines her expertise and detail-oriented knowledge to produce creative, quality teaching games and aids.

https://ultimatemusictheory.com/about-ultimate-music-theory/

8

IF THE SHOE FITS, WEAR IT

Paul Myatt and Gillian Erskine
Australia

Superstars? Us? Really?

Coming from the 'Land of the Tall Poppy Syndrome', Australia, where it just doesn't do to 'get too big for your boots', thinking of ourselves as superstars made both of us feel uncomfortable.

Like a pair of beautiful Jimmy Choo shoes with their soft luxurious uppers and kick-ass red leather soles that shout "Superstar!" Even though they may be a little too high to be comfortable, they do make us feel like a superstar when we wear them. And just for the record, Paul feels the same about an Armani suit.

What drove us to passionately pursue our dream over twenty-seven years and never give up even though we could have many times? Well, it all started when we were children but for different reasons.

Gillian's Story

I often say "I survived" my early years at piano. I could very well have given up many times. Lessons were arduous and practice was boring but there was no escape. My mother, who had regretted quitting piano as a child, was determined I wasn't going to do the same.

I loathed Wednesday afternoons when my heavily powdered and perfumed piano teacher arrived at our home to teach my brother and me. The only good thing about it was the chocolate-coated mint slice cookies and icy cold tangy pineapple juice we had for afternoon tea.

In the rare event that a lesson went well, which meant I didn't get yelled at, wrapped across the knuckles with her biro, given lines, or reduced to tears - I developed a "lucky dress' theory and believed that having magical qualities, this one was the one to wear next week!

My piano teacher was just a woman of her time, and many have endured a similar experience. Luckily for me, she retired when I was about ten, and my next teacher was very cool and nurtured my interest in music with fancy arrangements that made me feel awesome.

When I started teaching piano, I vowed and declared there must be a better way and there ignited a burning desire to find it.

. . .

Paul's Story

I had an eclectic piano upbringing, not having my first formal piano lesson till the age of fifteen. When I think back, I just always loved music. When my parents finally acquiesced and bought me an instrument it was an electronic organ which came with a box of music and tapes. Living in the country and moving frequently with my dad's job as a regional bank manager, there weren't a lot of teachers around, so I taught myself.

My earliest career dream was to make a living playing piano. At nineteen an opportunity unveiled that I could not refuse. I was a waiter in a hotel and the pianist in the restaurant was going on vacation. Management knew I was a music student and asked me to audition.

I did the audition with the belief that I could get the job, and I did. At that moment, panic set in as I only knew two pieces and I needed another two hours and fifty-four minutes of music, but that's another story.

All I can say is thank goodness for that box of music that came with the organ, as my self-teaching had led to developing a good ear and chord playing skills. As fortune would have it, I then became the pianist at David Jones, a department store (like Macy's or Harrods).

The story continues...

. . .

Gillian and Paul both owned successful music schools on different sides of the river in Brisbane but had never met until... one day whilst Paul was playing in the department store, he was introduced to Gillian by her husband who knew Paul. Little did they know that they were to become like family to each other and grow something amazing. It hasn't always been smooth sailing and there have been some tough times and big lessons learned along the way.

Stumbling first steps by Paul and Gillian

Our business consultant told us that the first step to our big dream of growing an international network was to show our system worked in another state. So late in the school year, we purchased and rebadged an existing music school with around 200 students and ten teachers in Sydney, ninety minutes fly time away.

Everything seemed to be going along fine until the new year when many teachers decided to move on for one reason or another. This left us the expenses of large premises and dwindling students. We were bleeding financially and the job of finding and training so many new teachers felt overwhelming. We could have very easily closed the doors, and no one would ever know... except us. Neither of us had ever failed at anything and didn't want this to be our first.

After some soul searching, we realised that this was an opportunity to breathe our energy and culture into the school so it could be reborn and flourish. This would take one of us.

. . .

Paul said, "I'll fly."

Gillian said, "What?"

He said, "I'll fly every week and spend half my time there and half in Brisbane."

With a major upheaval to his life and business, Paul began spending half the week in Sydney whilst Gillian focussed on supporting the rest of the small network back home.

The Sydney school started to thrive. We attracted a wonderful team of teachers and when we sold it a couple of years later it had over 500 students. What could have been a disaster became a success on many levels. One Sydney teacher decided to open another Forte School in Sydney and a young teacher at her school was inspired to open her own school in Melbourne several years later. This school today is one of the largest and most successful schools in the Forte group with around 900 students and has helped the owner achieve many of her own personal dreams. By holding onto our vision through the ups and downs and highs and lows over the years our 'superstar' has risen, fuelled by the burning desire to change the way music is taught. We still get excited when we think about what if we could help teachers engage and keep more students to keep learning music? What brilliant impact would that make on the lives of others as more children go on to enjoy the lifelong pleasure of playing music.

Remember if the shoe fits, wear it proudly.

Author Bio:

Gillian Erskine and Paul Myatt, founders of Forte School of Music, Forte Accredited Teacher Program and Piano Teaching Success help piano teachers attract, keep and teach more students to grow their income and have more fun teaching music.

https://pianoteachingsuccess.com

9

THE CROOKED PATH TO OWNING THE STAGE

Cate Friesen
Canada

Fourteen years into my career as a singer-songwriter I experienced debilitating stage fright for the first time. That magic moment of picking up my guitar, taking the stage, and raising my voice in song suddenly filled me with dread instead of excitement. I started forgetting lyrics and fumbling for the right chords. I was no longer present in the music or with my audience. I couldn't wait for it to be over so everyone would stop looking at me and expecting something that I couldn't give. I couldn't remember what it was I had to offer and why I had fought so hard to be on this stage.

That's one of the reasons the word 'superstar' almost stopped me from writing this chapter. I don't climb on the concert stage any more, and I never attained wide recognition, prominence, or the reputation of exceptional talent in the first place.

. . .

But choosing a career as a singer-songwriter for almost fifteen years taught me, in so many ways, how to be a superstar in my own life, to truly remember who I am, and what I have to offer this world. And that story starts in a farmhouse in southern Manitoba.

"Remember who you are," Dad would say to me and my older sisters whenever we left the house. He was the minister of the biggest church in our small Mennonite community. I heard: "Remember to be the Mennonite minister's good daughter." I was the president of the church youth group. I sang in the choir and got straight A's. I wore beige. Secretly, I dreamt of writing songs and touring the world with my guitar, but I signed up for occupational therapy instead. I could be of service. I was the first kid in my family to graduate from university. My dad was so proud.

I lasted about a year and a half working in a hospital. And then I packed up my guitar and headed east in a blue two-door hatchback. By my mid-twenties I was wearing green Doc Martens with purple laces. I worked odd jobs by day and wrote songs and played music in bars and coffee houses by night. But I hung on to that occupational therapy license just in case this music thing didn't work out. That year, when it was time to pay up, I didn't renew it. I was jumping into this music career with both feet. Exhilarating!

Then I mustered my courage to call my dad. "I just gave up my OT license," I announced over the phone line.

"I'll pay it!" said Dad.

"But it's not really about the money," I said. "I have found something I really want to do."

"You are throwing it all away?" he asked. And no amount of explaining could make him give me his blessing – and I really wanted that.

But in that moment – and it felt like for the first time – I understood what it meant to remember who I am, not who someone else thought I should be. I took off the yoke of remembering to be a minister's daughter. Instead, 'remember who you are' became my true north, my compass.

So, here I was at twenty-five years old, making a living as a songwriter and a performer. I learned pretty quickly that there's no one right way to climb the music ladder and no sure-fire equation of sweat, investment, and talent. It's what I call a crooked path: you need to stay alert, hold on to that compass – not with a tight grip, but with an open heart. Without an open heart you can't write and perform.

It was so easy to be distracted by some elusive measure of success like the number of people who came to shows and bought my CDs. I was often lured into measuring worth in applause, the size of venues, and favourable reviews. But I found my compass when I was truly present on stage, in song, voice, and story. In those moments, I remembered who I was and that I had something to offer up to the world that was uniquely mine. Then it wasn't the applause that mattered but the genuine connection that happened between me and the audience.

For as long as I could remember, even before I worked as a musician full time, the stage was my place. I wrote songs and sang them because it was the best way to express myself in the world and to connect with others. And when that stage fright kicked in, I was lost. Who was I, and why was I here, when I wasn't writing songs and performing?

It was a rough road for the next few years, but I found my place again on a different stage, in radio. It offered me a way to lift up other people's stories. It was another powerful way to connect.

Radio also offered a straighter road to success. I found myself at fifty-four with a leadership position and a good salary at our national public broadcaster. But once again, I had lost my way, my remembering, my compass. And as with that stage fright years ago, my body was screaming at me to leave.

I had to take three deep breaths before I hit 'call' on my cell phone to talk to my manager. I needed to be sure my voice was steady when I said, "I am leaving CBC."

"What are you going to do?" he asked.

"Storytelling and Capacity Building." I enunciated those words like they were capitalized – and like I knew what I was talking about. I had no business plan, a vague idea about story workshops, and a heart that was shouting an emphatic yes! I was remembering who I was and stepping back on that crooked path. That path has taken me from occupational therapy to touring across Canada as a singer-songwriter, to making radio documentaries, and launching shows for CBC. Now I work with others to help them discover and tell their stories that build connections and to remember who they are and why they do what they do.

. . .

When you truly remember who you are and can live from that place, your definition of recognition, of prominence, of the big stage, might change. One day you might look around and see yourself working with a community group, or sitting across from someone talking about their story, or writing a chapter in a book about how you climbed to stardom on a crooked path... and you'll find yourself on the stage where you were meant to be.

Author Bio:

Cate Friesen is a keynote presenter, award-winning CBC producer, documentary maker and performer. Cate helps you discover and tell your essential stories to move your work forward and inspire others. She's a story practitioner, gifted trainer and inspiring coach.

https://www.thestorysource.ca/

10

THE RISE TO SUPERSTAR

Ray St. Germain Jr.
USA

What is a superstar? Most people think of superstars as athletes or performers who have reached the pinnacle of achievement and are known worldwide. A superstar is also anyone who is very prominent or successful. My wife will tell you that I have an extremely "healthy" self-esteem and certainly "act" like a superstar in my everyday life. Well, that may be true to a certain extent, but success to me is NOT the end result, it's the journey. The following is my journey to success and rise to superstar in business, music, education, and most importantly life.

My journey started when I decided that I wanted to make a career in music. This journey brought me to Nashville, where I live today just outside the city with my beautiful wife (and best friend), talented daughter, and two dogs Roxy and Pebbles.

The journey was never easy and was certainly the roller coaster ride of my life. I had an extremely successful band called Dixie Devils that played to sold out crowds and packed houses all over downtown Nashville. We were the house band at the iconic nightclub Tootsie's Orchid Lounge and Legend's Corner. We had regular fans coming to our shows like John Rich of Big and Rich, Michael Peterson, Eric Heatherly, and countless others. The future was bright, and we were the hottest band in Nashville. We were invited to Sony Studios and were courted by a big producer who had been watching what we were doing and looking to sign us to a major record deal. When this did not transpire, we opted for a new deal with an independent label out of Los Angeles. We finally had our big break, or so we thought. I could fill all of the details, emotions, side-stories, and heartbreak in an entire book on its own (Perhaps I will start this journey one day.). The bottom line is the funding got pulled from the label entirely and we started down a road of losing band members, overindulgence, and typical in-house squabbles. It was at this point I knew I had to reinvent myself or my career was going to be cut extremely short. This was when I realized I knew all about music but knew nothing about the music business.

The best parts of being on a journey are the choices we make along the way. Decision time. I knew that I had to get my tail back into school and learn everything I could about business. I wound up returning to college and getting my Associate Degree, Bachelor Degree in Business Management, and finally my Master of Business Administration (MBA). It was years of hard work and determination, but I did it. Of course, I kept playing during that time with my new band the Music Row

Rejects, with Randy Carie from the Dixie Devils. We have played all over the country and toured Australia. I also met a great songwriter and long-time friend Anderson Layne. We formed Anderson Layne and the Killer Saints and write, produce, and perform original rock and roll music which is available on iTunes, Spotify, and countless other streaming services. I am also in the process of recording a solo album with several long-time musical friends which will include several original songs, as well as songs from my dad, Ray St. Germain Sr., Anderson Layne, and Mike Reno of Loverboy.

While becoming an education superstar, I not only got married, but the best thing I ever did was become a father. I have made it my mission to be a superstar dad, and I am there for everything my daughter has done and will do. She is an amazing singer, songwriter, artist, actress, and now dancer. Yes, I'm a certified superstar dance dad. She is on a competitive dance team, and I will be there for every meet, as long as the good Lord is willing. It's at this point of my journey that life on the road touring is not the most appealing option. It's hard enough trying to balance two different bands, recording a solo album, a very successful sales career, being a superstar dance dad, and trying to be a superstar husband. I figured why not add another journey to the mix.

I am also the owner of Rayzr Custom Engraving. I thought it would be cool to have another "side gig" so I bought a business. It's been wonderful, since I consider myself a workaholic; it allows me another avenue to be creative and open another stream of revenue. Like I said, success is not the destination, it's the journey and I'm right in the middle of mine.

As I reflect on my superstar life, I am so thankful for everything I have accomplished, and most importantly failed at in life. I learn from my failures and turn them into inspirations. Many people ask me, "I want to come to Nashville to shop around my songs for a couple months. Got any advice?" I always say the same thing. "Save your money. Unless you are ready and willing to move here permanently, and commit, don't bother." This may sound harsh, but the bottom line is this: If you want to be a superstar, commit. Do everything you can to achieve your goals. Start with small goals but be sure to achieve them. If you fail, learn from it and keep going. Your journey to superstar will have forks in the road and you have to be ready and willing to take a turn when you have to.

I will always have music. It's in me, and I couldn't get away from it if I wanted to and believe me, I've tried. I love it too much. But I love my family more. This is my rise to superstar, what's yours?

In closing, I recently lost a very dear friend that I've known since the sixth grade. Aimee Allen Kirk, my self-proclaimed biggest fan. The last thing she said to me was this, "Thank you, Punkin. I do feel better! Tell your sweet family I said hello. Maybe one day you will look out from a stage and see my shiny round face grinning back at you! Have a great weekend."

Aimee my dearest friend, I will see your beautiful shining face every time I take a stage. Thank you for being my Superstar.

Author Bio:

Ray St. Germain Jr. MBA is a lead guitar player/singer/songwriter, and Co-founder of Anderson Layne and the Killer Saints, The Music Row Rejects and currently working on a Solo Album. Ray is the Owner of Rayzr Custom Engraving and lives in Nashville with his wife and daughter.

https://www.facebook.com/musicrowrejects

11

KEEP GOING

Doreen Hall
USA

Keep Going!
"A quitter never wins, and a winner never quits." ~ Napoleon Hill

"Nothing in this world can take the place of persistence. Talent will not: nothing is more common than unsuccessful men with talent." ~ Calvin Coolidge

Do you want to be a superstar? That is, do something amazing and important? Do you want to make a difference in the world? Do you want to achieve your dreams and be successful?

The great news is that you can. I am doing it, and so can you. In this chapter I am going to give you my two cents on what it means to be a superstar and how to get there.

What is a superstar anyway? By definition, a superstar is someone who has a huge following and enormous popularity.

But I define a superstar as anyone who does something meaningful, no matter how big or small. You can be a superstar in your own right, in your own circle, by doing your best to serve others and create something extraordinary. By helping others, touching people's hearts, and creating beauty.

Here is how I am working toward my superstar goals; my hope is that some of these ideas will help you too. Every one of us is different, so take what you like and leave the rest. Trust that you can find your unique path to becoming a superstar.

Have a vision.

Imagine - I love this word. Imagine what you really want to achieve. Hold that thought in your mind. Imagine yourself in the future doing exactly what you would love to be doing. My vision was to be a composer, a teacher, and a good musician. I want to do something that would last and make a difference to others in the music world.

Put your goals in writing.

Would you like to write a book, start a business, or learn something new? Write it down and post it where you can see it every day. In my experience, putting goals in writing brings them to life. Written words give me something concrete to look at. Having written goals helps me stay focused.

Get ready to work.

Of course, many people have great ideas but great ideas in and of themselves won't get you anywhere if you aren't willing to work hard. So, you must be willing to roll up your sleeves and get to work. After all, if you're trying to do more than the average person, you will have to work harder.

Do a brain dump.

I am a composer, poet, and writer. When I feel inspired, I grab a pen and my "thinking book" (a notebook or manuscript book) and write whatever pops into my mind. I use a pen because I never erase an idea no matter how silly it may seem at the time. I have found that ideas beget more ideas. When I have written everything I can think of, I start a new page and begin refining.

For me, the first part of this process takes an hour or two because I need time to let my creativity begin to flow. However, I know there are other people who have moments of creative inspiration throughout the day. These people keep a pad or voice recorder handy so they can save their ideas. Be mindful of what works for you and do it consistently.

Learn, learn, learn.

One of the biggest challenges for me when I started publishing music was that I didn't know what I didn't know. I wrote lots of music, and built a website but in the beginning, no one noticed. I didn't know how to get my music out there. I had (and still have) a lot to learn about marketing, advertising, and business building. I am also always learning to be a better musician, teacher, and composer. I strive to learn about the latest technology so that I can deliver the very best content.

Surround yourself with the right people.

I made it a priority to find the right people to work with, positive people who know what they are doing. People who are encouraging but are willing to tell me the truth. I need accurate feedback in order to move ahead and improve.

Get back up.

If you want to be a superstar, get ready to deal with setbacks. Setbacks are inevitable. Sometimes mistakes are small, a typo, or something like that. Sometimes people make negative comments. Websites are prone to technical difficulty from time to time. Sometimes, bigger things happen like a total website crash, failed product launch, or a less than stellar performance. I get knocked down regularly, but I get up again. If you want to be a superstar, you must keep moving ahead. You may need a break from time to time, but you must not quit.

Enjoy the process and be flexible.

What good is it to be a superstar if you're not happy? You

need to do something you like while finding and maintaining balance and joy while you are doing it. It is also important to realize that the road to success is often full of twists and turns. While it's important to keep your eyes on the prize, it's also helpful to be flexible and open to new concepts and ways of doing things. Love what you are doing and keep going.

What am I doing now?

I am still hard at work on my website palomapiano.com which has thousands of pages of music and other resources for piano teachers and students. I also am busy running a piano teaching studio and playing the piano professionally. I try to start each day by being grateful for all the beautiful things that life has to offer. Family and friends, nature, and the arts to name a few. How do I try to be a superstar? Just by being a little bit better, kinder, and more loving each day.

Author Bio:

Doreen Hall is the composer/creator of piano music and teaching resources at palomapiano.com. She has written two books The Happiest Piano Teacher in Town" and "The Ultimate Preschool Piano Activities Book" both available at amazom.com

www.palomapiano.com

12

PIANO TEACHING - SPREADING JOY AND PASSION

Karen Hedges
USA

I have always loved to play the piano. It's a passion for me. I was never into sports or dance; it was music - singing, playing piano, and playing the guitar. As a young girl, I knew I wanted to teach but didn't know what I wanted to teach. I started teaching piano soon after I got married. My husband, George, and his family opened Shiloh Music Center in 1974. Right after I started accepting students, I fell in love with teaching. I found my passion.

Over the years, we have offered music lessons of all kinds. At that time, we had two small studios, one for piano and one for guitar. Fast forward to 2021, we have nine studios, seventeen teachers, and teach lessons on many different instruments. I kept the vision of having several studios, teachers, and lots of students learning music. It has been a dream come true to be able to teach music to so many students in Mt. Juliet and the surrounding areas. Many of our students over the years have become music teachers, band directors, and are working in the music industry as performers or behind the scenes. Even after forty-six years of teaching, I still love to watch the lightbulb glow when a student finally understands eighth note rhythms, playing with dynamics, playing musically, and even learning where middle C is. I also learned along the way that each student teaches me something new. I am organized in my teaching, following several different method courses with my students. My students have made me the teacher I am today. I have continued to study everything about teaching I can find. I have attended several piano teacher conferences, like the National Conference on Keyboard Pedagogy and many publishers showcases. I also belong to the Music Teachers National Association, Nashville Area Music Teachers Association, National Guild of Piano Teachers, and Nashville Association of Guild Piano Teachers, a local group of teachers in the Nashville area. There is a wealth of information from other teachers and composers who love to share their experiences. I encourage all teachers, new or seasoned, to continue learning and to share their knowledge with their students and other teachers. I love to support the piano teaching community in our area to become better teachers and to mentor other teachers.

I have been a member of the National Guild of Piano Teachers for twenty-five plus years and am currently the chairperson for our local center. When I first joined the guild, my first couple of years was a bit overwhelming. I feel that joining the guild and entering my students was the best thing I could do for my teaching. The students get 'graded' on their performance and we receive positive feedback from the judge. I became a better teacher and love to cheer my students on as their 'piano coach' to do the best they can do. I would have to say some of the highlights of my career have been all the students I have taught over the forty-six years of my career. Not only have I taught them to play the piano, but we have also shared experiences with several performance opportunities each year. We perform in recitals, play for senior citizen communities, and perform for other events in our city.

It brings me great joy to watch my students perform with confidence and share their love of music. One of my huge goals of teaching is to instill the love of music into my students' lives so they will have a lifelong passion for piano. I have students who have taken lessons with me for twelve or more years. I get to watch them grow up, be a part of their lives as they grow, and watch them grow into young adults. To be able to watch former students go on to teach music in public and private schools, become band directors, and to open their own piano studios is proof I am achieving my goal. I have mentored lots of new teachers. Two of our newest piano teachers at our music store are former students of mine. It was such a proud moment to add them to our staff of teachers.

The highlight of my career happened Sept. 30, 2021, when I was inducted into the Steinway Music Teacher Hall of Fame. Our local Steinway Gallery in Nashville, TN nominated me for the award. When I received the call, I was excited and honored. I had to put my phone on speaker so George could hear everything. After teaching for forty-six years, and loving what I do, I was so honored and humbled to receive this award. It's an honor to be recognized for my long career. My husband and I were flown to NY for the banquet, induction ceremony, and concert. There were a total of forty-four teachers inducted into the Hall of Fame this year. At the induction ceremony, we were all awarded a beautiful certificate which now hangs in my studio. We were treated to a very nice dinner and concert. The next day, we toured the Steinway Factory. The first thing we saw was the Wall of Fame with our names listed. It was an uplifting feeling. Our local newspaper featured an article about my award. On the day the paper came out, one of my sweet students came in for her lesson with her copy of the paper and asked me to autograph her copy. I felt like a celebrity superstar. Follow your dreams, achieve your goals, and have fun along the way as you find your passion and joy.

Author Bio:

Karen Hedges and her husband own and operate Shiloh Music Center. She is an accomplished musician, pianist, and teacher whose guiding principle is to instill a life-long love of music. Karen was inducted into the Steinway Music Teacher Hall of Fame on September 30, 2021.

https://shilohmusiccenter.com

13

MUSIC WAS A CALLING THAT LED THE WAY

Shumaila Hemani
Canada

In a sudden rush after a work-out when I was thirteen, I had taken a lead pencil and scribbled on my wall. When I left home as a late teenager and my mother missed me, she would visit my room and notice my walls. But now, the walls had been repainted, yet the emotions and memories are still alive and present. Years ago, when I had come for a visit from my studies in Canada, my mother asked me what it meant. I asked her to read it aloud. "I'll leave this dungeon, soon." I heard her say. She was confused, and I stayed silent feeling too embarrassed to share with her how keen I was to leave home because I never felt like I belonged.

COVID-19 forced me to return to my home country in March 2020. I was on a voyage working within a Music Faculty at the Semester at Sea's Spring 2020 voyage. On my return, I confronted the misfit teenager who dropped out of college twice. What had kept me going were the words of a mentor, "Your journey will make space in this world for people who do not fit the mold." My journey in music and songwriting gave me a space to express a part of me that is not accessible to people around me. It helped me to breathe while giving visibility to people from my culture and community.

Our voices are our most sacred instruments. It helps us to connect with others and allows us to heal from the hurt, pain, and disappointment that we have suffered. There have been many times when I felt my voice subdued and silenced. This was the norm during my teenage years and early twenties.

I was too shy to express my opinions in class at the elite college I studied at because of the fear of rejection. Sometimes, I was called out within the friends' circle as the only person who had not spoken a word. I was afraid to talk because I did not have the space to be myself, and my words always pricked someone. There was no room for more pain. So, I embraced silence.

When I perform, my eyes and posture are closed because I am trying to create a space that I do not think exists for people like me in this world. We could be movers and shakers but most of what we give to the world is taken for granted, under-appreciated, and under-valued. But in listening to our calling, we find new ways to connect and live meaningfully.

Since 2015, my dark spots became more intense. I was a doctoral student, then. I continued moving towards my calling, creating new works and confronting many challenges. Five years later, in 2020, my song "Anticipating" was featured in the Cross-Canada Tour for Suicide Prevention Awareness and Hope.

Music is visceral and it makes us connect. Many hearts are young with desire, aspiration, and dream to pursue what makes them feel more alive and joyful. Yet, that which we love is also what we are afraid to move towards if our conditioning has been to deny who we are and be dismissive of our dreams.

My calling in music led me on a path towards absolute self-acceptance.

Studying Islam and its diverse interpretations have given me several opportunities to interact with voice cultures in Muslim contexts. I have traveled to the roof of the world, Badakhshan, Tajikistan, and collected oral narratives of males and females who preserved their religious recitation called the *maddoh* during the Soviet era. In Edmonton, Alberta, I interacted with the Afghan diaspora to learn how they are continuing their tradition of singing qasida in Canada. I am currently writing a book based on my dissertation about the Sufi tradition of the Shah jo Raag in Pakistan.

Yet, there is a dimension of vocality that is beyond its materiality and is rather related to the visibility it brings to our place of vulnerability. In 2019, when I graduated with a Doctor of Philosophy in Music from the University of Alberta, I felt that in representing culture, my scholarly subjectivity was not able to bring audibility to the voice that began the journey in music in the first place. I was fortunate that a music residency in Toronto led to a new path of recording original songs that bring audibility to my personal journey because even though dwelling on this journey may be insubstantial for my scholarly contributions, it gave me a space to be vulnerable and share a part of me that I would not be able to share with my family or the scholarly community.

And the why for creation is not only my person anymore. I have learned from my listeners how the melody and lyrics of anticipating and living with purpose have empowered them with a space to imagine a new path. Here, I am referring to my brother who was once my biggest critic. When I was a teenager, I was asked to put the volume down and not to sing when I was with my family, but here he was, playing my songs on a loudspeaker, and finding his way forward from a heartbreak.

Music showed me an alternate way to live, a way that was truer to my heart's calling. To see my expressivity giving another person license to follow their calling sets free even more birds inside of me. To see someone being empowered by these songs and overcoming challenges means that what we consider "personal" is never restricted to one person. What connects with us does have the power to resonate with many more out there. And if we all allow ourselves a place to be and breathe, will not life be so much more meaningful and fuller? We are holding different parts of us together because we are afraid to fall apart. Embracing that life is a process, a work-in-progress. I realize that sometimes it is okay to be confused about where this is all going and not have everything figured out. Also, it is okay to fall apart, reach out for help, and then find the courage and strength to re-build which permits us to stop trying so hard to fit into the mold. It allows us to step in our power, take charge, and set out on a journey towards a more fulfilling tomorrow. For me, it is my calling in music that has led the way.

Author Bio:

Shumaila Hemani, Ph.D. in Music from the University of Alberta is an Alberta-based Sufi singer-songwriter, acousmatic composer and Music Faculty. Her award-winning composition Perils of Heavy Rainfall and song: Anticipating have been featured in Canada.

https://www.shumailahemani.com/

14

CREATING SUPERSTAR STUDENTS

David A. Jones
UK

This is about the pathway to your 'superstardom,' not mine.

I aim to show you how you may already be on your route to epic success. Or maybe, with the simplest tweaks, you can be. But bear in mind that the term 'superstar' is relative.

To roughly paraphrase Syndrome from *The Incredibles*, when everyone is a superstar, no one is. As much as Syndrome is the villain in the movie, the strive for human advancement has existed since our earliest predecessors advanced from amoeba.

This chapter bullets three key steps that were fundamental in leading me to my dream career and how you can do the same. As I've said so many times before, if I can do it, then anyone can.

STEP 1 - I identified, created, developed, and packaged my passion to share with others.

We are all unique. We approach everyday activities with individuality. If you have a passion and you can present it with your own style, you'll find others who resonate with your message too. They will want to learn about your passion from you.

Example: I loved teaching the three-to-six-year age range from the beginning. Yes, our school teaches to beyond Degree level, but the energy and excitement of little ones for our music lessons is an inspiration. This was especially true when witnessing the immense benefits of music education within that young age group.

When taught via an approved system, you are nurturing all the benefits of music in your students: increased confidence, coordination, self-expression, concentration, memory skills, problem solving etc. The list is extensive and globally proven.

I am helping others in an area that I truly love and believe in. If you can share your passion and knowledge, then you can do the same. If you follow the steps to get there, you'll do what you love for a living and never have to do a day of 'work' in your life.

STEP 2 - We used an officially recognised system to help us to deliver STEP 1, putting our own unique spin on it.

There are processes that others have proved are successful. Do the research and use the discoveries and platforms of others to jump-start your journey. This also boosts your speed of progress. You can then bring your individual flavour to the party.

Example: We started to use the London College of Music Exams (LCME) at our fledgling music school. We were therefore using a recognised name which gave us added credibility. To advance our position further, we spent years creating, testing, and refining our course systems for the continuous development of our teachers and students.

We'd taken traditional music education and presented it in a more intuitive, immediately applicable way - ideal for a wider range of students and their learning styles. We pitched our new take on music education back to LCME who agreed with our approach, and we were uniquely commissioned to write our "Presto" courseware.

STEP 3 - We pushed further and began to create our individual stamp on how we delivered 1 and 2.

We wanted to revolutionise the way real music was taught making it more fun, inspirational and immediate in the way all students progressed.

I talk about how we gained unique LCME recognition for our courses and how we actually achieved our core goals in our teacher training systems. However, in summary, our key objectives were:

1. Use our unique approach to create separate courses for specific age groups which dovetailed seamlessly together, taking students from the age of three to pro musicianship and beyond Degree Level. It would include all official certifications along the way and encompass additional composition from day one, song writing, recording, and music production coaching.

2. Create loveable cartoon characters that would connect with the youngest of our target age group yet entertain the whole family. This way, a child would learn through 'edutainment' and the embodiment of Teamwork which is at the core of everything we do.

3. Create training systems for other teachers so they could share in our discoveries, building their own music school businesses by leveraging our courses recognition.

We only really have three main resources at our disposal: time, energy and money. In essence, any other resource falls into these three categories. If you don't have one or two of these, then you need to use the other(s) to leverage your progress. Above all, save yourself time, energy and money.

SYSTEM

You need a system that will guide you: a route map with a proven track record. Learning and developing skills along life's journey is important, but nobody reinvents the wheel when designing new transport.

We used the knowledge, resources, experience and guidance from others to hugely accelerate our own business. Why spend months, or even years, trying to work something out when others have already mapped it out. You can train with them, therefore leapfrogging your progress paying only a couple of hundred dollars to save years of pain.

Don't waste the most valuable resource you have - you can replace most things, but not time.

Those who fail tend not to have a plan, or they fail to execute any plan they do have. They do not have clear steps laid out as to what to do, and when to do it. If you have a clear route map from where you are to where you want to be, then your chance of success is increased exponentially.

There are lots of great systems out there - this isn't a "we only recommend that you use our course" pitch - though you would be welcome to check us out.

SUMMARY

If my Presto team and I have been lifted to anywhere near "Superstar" status then it is purely the teamwork of staff, students, parents, and carers who have raised us there. I aim to focus on our Presto Music School family as a whole. I'm not trying to raise myself up to superstardom, I never have.

My aim has always been to get our students to learn faster, with a deeper understanding and achieve higher golas than they expected. To help others work toward self-improvement with a 'can do' attitude is the embodiment of our #PositivelyPresto way.

So, back to Syndrome. I don't feel that I'm super at all. I'm just on a mission to share the massive benefits and immense fun of music. In doing so, we raise the bar of what normal is. So, I see it the other way round: Let us teach future generations to all be superstars.

Author Bio:

David A Jones (BAPMR) : Director of Presto Music School, LCME recognised Course Creator, Co-Creator of the Musical TV Series "Rhythm Warriors" produced by Emofront and Presto Music Production in association with Sparky Animation Studios.

https://online.prestomusicschool.co.uk/businessbuilder

15

MUSIC AS CONNECTION

Dominique Levack
Spain

My early beginnings as a piano player and composer are documented in the international bestselling book *The Power of Why: Why 25 Musicians Composed a Legacy*.

The opportunity to have been introduced to the piano at the age of four by a Boogie Woogie player influenced the course of my life. If only I could find Malt now and thank him for a life of music. Little did either of us know in those hours, weeks, and months he looked after me at the piano, while my mum was studying fashion at college back in the 1970's, that his brilliant improvisational playing would inspire me so deeply. It's in these singular moments of musical connection that you can never predict how profoundly they affect others. As the years have gone by, I have enjoyed many moments of musical connection as a performer, songwriter, composer, and DJ but nothing has compared to the reaction music gets in a therapeutic environment, as an intervention.

I was led towards music therapy by a dear friend who suffers from bipolar disorder, which is a chronic mental health disorder. She attended a wonderful day centre in West Sussex for people who have a host of similar mental health conditions, including depression, addictions, and various physical disabilities. I had run a series of singing and songwriting courses at a local music studio, which she attended, and she suggested I take these courses and delivered them at the centre.

I was unsure whether I was going to be able to cope with the service users' needs, but I took her advice and contacted the manager. Soon afterwards, I found myself running courses and a community choir started to form, with little performances at summer fairs and Christmas concerts. The group wrote songs and recorded them, created artwork, and produced CDs to raise money for the centre.

I found myself working with women who were suffering from agoraphobia and alcoholism in the same room, focusing together on music, leaving their difficulties at the door. Music found a way to include and absorb each and every one of them, and bring joy. I remember one particular session we were visiting the local recording studio and one of our group, a partially deaf lady, started to sing with us because she felt the vibrations of the music through the bass amp and electric piano. She sang "Let It Be" with such joy and hope loud and proud that we all had tears in our eyes. It was a moment of connection.

. . .

I wanted to learn more, so I went back to study for a Masters in Music Health & Society, at the age of forty-six having gained a place at Nordoff Robbins in London. This was my greatest challenge. Having left school in the 80s with a bunch of A levels, I avoided University at eighteen choosing instead to go on tour with a rock band around Europe. So off I went to study on a master's course totally without academic training - the oldest woman on the course and older than most of the tutors.

It was a tough ride. It took me back to myself by challenging my musical abilities, forcing me to dig deep, then deeper still, to listen, to watch, and to observe without judgement. Then I needed to reflect, to respond, to critique my own work, again and again and again. My musicality was exposed for all to hear.

I finished the master's early, without choice, close to a breakdown and with gallstones. However, with the learning and discipline I have gained, I am able to work with different people across society and make this musical connection a career.

Case studies over the years are little miracles of musical connection. I find clients come to me, either by referral or by chance and fate. Once I was asked to run an improvisational choir at a festival in a large tepee with fifty wonderful adults of all ages, shapes and sizes in a giant circle singing or vocalising in some way using sounds that meant something to them. It was so joyful and uplifting; we all felt energised afterwards. Whilst packing away, a young woman with her child came up to me in tears. Her daughter was seven years old and had been a selective mute for the past three years, until the singing. Somehow in the circle she had found her voice in our safe and musically held space.

This is the power of music.

I find this path very rewarding and would recommend music therapy as a career and as an intervention for anyone who seeks this connection. I have seen music crack open a path of connection into the brains of people with dementia, Parkinson's, Huntington's Disease, spectrum disorders, profound learning difficulties, Down Syndrome, and on and on. I have never found a person that music cannot reach.

In my final days at Nordoff Robbins, I wrote this poem, which was published in *Leading Note*, a specialised publication for Music Therapists in the UK.

A Riddle. What am I?

With great expectation and open horizons
    An unending journey of old,
    and like Boudicca the roads never clear,
  Yet dreams held inside do unfold.

I chant with the others the fatherless mothers,
    who sacrifice much robbed of choice.
    And there in the silence I sing in the distance
    And meet the emotional voice.

. . .

Holding hands with the dying I honour their crying,
   I reach behind the eyes of the blind.
   I dance with the stories of heartbreak and glory
   and love them because they are mine.

With playful rhythm I mend broken children,
   Lifting their heads to the skies
   with soldiers I stand, as they march across lands
   Calling right by their side when they die.

What am I you ask?
   This hero of brass.
   An invisible blanket of magic.
   Let us worship this force, a universal source – my invisible love We call music.

Author Bio:

   Dominique works as a composer/songwriter and music specialist in the UK and Spain. A musical time traveller she especially enjoys working with voices. Using music therapy to connect, she enjoys working with challenging clients.

www.dominiquelevack.com

16

ENTREPRENEURIAL RESILIENCE

Rebecca Feathersone
Canada

I am a pretty regular person doing regular people's things for the majority of my life. I'm a mom of two small boys, I love dogs, hiking in the woods, and I've taught piano for over two decades. Like many piano teachers, I have a BA in Music. Nobody prepared me for the hurdles to be jumped when I took on the role of founder of a software company.

In March of 2020, I began preparations for securing funding to build a video conference platform built for music teachers to teach online. This vision that I had was not a simple one by any means. I wanted not only a basic video conference platform but a platform that was geared to music teachers and in particular children. I watched as my then six-year-old son struggled with online learning on traditional software as he stared at the screen and his grade one teacher desperately tried to engage her students. I wondered why there wasn't a platform that had equal access from both sides of the screen to interact with the teacher. Children are not meant to sit still and listen when they learn. They need a hands-on approach and interaction. This is how the idea for Musicology was born. The first interactive music platform specifically designed for child engagement.

So, here's the thing you often hear people say, "I want to make an app! Why isn't there an app for that? It would be so easy." It's not. The years of 2020-2021 were the hardest times of my life. It was harder than being a new mom with a newborn and equally exhausting. Why is it so hard, you ask? Let me tell you. It's not as simple as building something, and it just works on every device imaginable. You must build the platform for each device and then make them speak to each other. If there is a bug (and there are always bugs), fixing it could create a new bug, and it goes on and on forever. It doesn't just cost a few thousand dollars either. It's hundreds of thousands of dollars.

When you build a software company, you first start with a very detailed business plan and financial projections (which are really just a bunch of made-up numbers). Then, you secure funding either from private investors or a bank that supports start-ups or both. In our case, we did both. So, on top of the bank breathing down your neck to make sure they can make their money back and then some you also have real live people who want the same thing. No pressure, eh? Most start-ups die within the first year. It's easy to have an idea, but it's certainly not easy to keep that idea alive and thriving.

Being an entrepreneur navigating a tech start-up through a niche industry is no easy task and although there are many organizations that support start-ups (especially woman owned start-ups), there is literally zero support in the music industry. It's all business, and let's face it, we just don't learn that in music school. So, on top of launching a global software company, running my own music school, and caring for my family, I had to learn how to negotiate the business world doing every course that I could fit into my schedule. In between educating myself, I was working on learning how to support our subscribers, learn content creation, and just get into a general rhythm and flow of things. I have to say, it's much better now, but boy, has this last year been a whirlwind.

When I first met my marketing director, he told me to be prepared for great amounts of stress once we launched and to keep my eyes wide open. He said that many CEOs end up in the hospital with heart conditions. In my experience, some people would approach me for money, others were angry because the app didn't have the specific feature they wanted, and some were vengeful because the platform didn't work the way they expected due to device or internet issues that were out of our control. Boy, was he right. One thing that no one told me was the scheming money-hungry world that business is. As teachers, we don't often think about money. We are happy to be making a difference in young people's lives and to be able to pay our bills. You hear about businesspeople gone bad on television shows but don't really experience it for the most part. Unfortunately for me, I received the full start-up experience - people you trusted who turn on you for greed. It's so disheartening and so humanly disappointing.

But do you know what, good has come out of these experiences: resiliency. To be resilient is to be able to withstand or recover quickly from difficult situations, and I would have to say that this is one of my top qualities. I always knew that I was resilient but never knew to what extent. Taking the glorious plunge to weather through whatever life threw at me during this journey has taught me to not only value myself but to also value and appreciate human beings even more. To be able to take all the ups and downs that are thrown your way and come out of it a stronger person, that is more knowledgeable, is a very valuable lesson. I would encourage each and every one of you to take that leap of faith and get back up when you get knocked down. See life challenges as an opportunity for growth and education. We teach young minds each and every day but we often forget that we as adults need to keep taking risks so we can also grow. Trust yourself and your vision. Trust good people around you. Learn from the negative and use that to fertilize your soul for the future. You are worth it. You deserve it. And remember, nothing ever lasts forever, and it always works out in the end.

Author Bio:

Rebecca Featherstone Founder & CEO of Musicology, a robust video conferencing platform designed to teach music online. She is a graduate of Mohawk College for Applied Arts (2000) and McMaster University BA in Music (2002) and owner of a multi-teacher studio.

www.musicology.ca

17

SUPER-STAR CREATOR

Ivy Leung
Hong Kong

Before 2008, there were just a few music competitions in Hong Kong. The famous ones were old fashioned. They provided a limited choice of music for candidates. The music was monotonous and demanding. It was evident that some of the students practiced the songs under pressure, so we could imagine they probably did not enjoy the music while they were practicing. Additionally, the old-fashioned organisations had no communication or cooperation with other potential organizations, so it seemed that everything was over when the competitions ended. They might have to wait and join another competition or examination. At that moment, I began to ask myself, "Is that the only way for students to participate in the music activities?"

As a music teacher, I believe every student has potential, and all they need is practice and having a professional stage on which to perform. That's why I have held a music competition since 2008. I believe that the winners of my competition are talented, they have incredible music to share, and they have the potential to become superstars through my music activities.

I am the chairperson of the Hong Kong registered charity music development association which holds music competitions and music overseas culture activities in Japan, Australia, and Taiwan.

I wanted to be a creator of superstars, so I designed my music competitions involving different groups for students to join. There were groups of pop music, syllabus from famous examinations, and their own choices. Therefore, there would be more comprehensive selections for them to play following their love of music. They could enjoy themselves while they were practicing. So, they would have better performances in the competitions or examinations. They would have a better way to show their strengths based on their own interests. Many young musicians participated in my events, including pianists, violinists, harpists, wind players, singers, and even some rare instrumentalists playing instruments such as the "Pai flute". I invited professional musicians to be the adjudicators, including music professors from university, composers, orchestral conductors, and experienced educators. The most valuable thing about music is to share. Music is a tool to communicate with people and bring people closer. Therefore, I started cooperating with many organisations like listed companies, theme parks, property management companies, theatres, and choirs. These organisations provided diverse activities and chances for my young musicians to perform.

Playing in theme parks and shopping malls provided a casual platform on which to perform. Like on Christmas, the students chose pop music, cartoon music ,and Christmas songs to play.

They dressed like princes or princesses and brought sweet music and love to the public.

When I was little, I saw some performers dressed beautifully and playing the piano on the stage. It inspired me to learn piano. Therefore, I believe that public performances will encourage more children to learn musical instruments. On the other hand, playing in theatres and concert halls is much more serious and professional. They could have more opportunities to play ensembles with professional orchestras and accompany the choirs. These opportunities would encourage students to practice more challenging and demanding pieces. But it was not just what I wanted, I had even bigger ambitions. I wanted the students in Hong Kong to have a broader scope. Therefore, I arranged my music events globally, including in Australia and in Okinawa, Japan. Students between Hong Kong and these two countries could have chances for cultural exchange. In the past few years, Hong Kong candidates have made friends with Australian and Japanese candidates during my music events in Australia and Japan.

Nowadays, using the Internet is becoming more popular. Also, because of the COVID 19 issue, I organised online events in which candidates could participate. For example, I invited professional musicians to hold some masterclasses. The speakers covered many different musical topics, like the strategy of practicing, history, music theory, composing, performance techniques and planning for examinations. Of course, I would not miss the chance to hold my music competitions, which I excel at, globally using an online platform. I put the performance videos from the candidates online. So, they could share their videos with their friends. The feedback from the participants, parents, and teachers was positive. They learned a lot from the events.

Additionally, the students were rewarded for their hard work. I am so happy that my events provided them with some amazing opportunities. In the past fourteen years, it was so lucky that a lot of mass media reported on our candidates' contributions to the music field. They received interviews from newspapers and TV shows. Their performances were broadcast on televisions and radios. Furthermore, their performances were recorded by charity organisations to publish DVDs. The DVDs were released for charitable purposes. My beloved winners certainly became superstars. They utilised their strengths and abilities to help people in need. They gave back to society. Sometimes, I am jealous of my students because I never had the same opportunities as they did as a child.

"Every day is different and improvised. Sometimes, a song can lead to a completely different adventure. You cannot control it."

When I was a child, I thought that music was simply playing an instrument. After completing my music degree and teaching for twenty-five years, I realized that music is not just playing an instrument, but also a door to the universe. I wish I could be wiser and stronger to contribute more to music. With music, there are no restrictions or limitations around the world. You can reach for the stars as high as you can.

Author Bio:

Ivy Leung CW, over twenty years teaching experience, chairperson of a HK registered charity music development association which holds music competitions and music overseas culture activities in Japan, Australia, and Taiwan.

www.hkget.com

18

SUCCESS IS YOUR STORY

William Montgomery
USA

As young children we consistently look towards the biggest names as ideals of what we want our lives to be. Whether it was Beethoven and his piano sonatas, the great Russian ballet composers (Stravinsky, Tchaikovsky, and Prokofiev), or Mahler and his gigantic symphonies, I would devote hours of my free time listening, analyzing, and imitating their styles.

One of my first compositions was a short symphonic work that was a compilation of samples of music taken from these great composers and combined in my way. I presented this piece to my first composition lesson. I thought it was a wonderful combination but within seconds, he said, "Have you ever heard of the great quote, 'good composers borrow, great composers steal'? Well, this piece is interesting but wouldn't pass as a great piece. Or a good piece." While this was a demoralizing moment for me, he then went on to discuss the quality of my handwriting (this was before computer programs such as Finale or Sibelius), the good transitions between the samples, and the rise and falls of the drama or tension. It would be a few more years of refinement but I eventually decided to follow up and take lessons with a local composition college professor. This would catapult me to follow my dream of being a composer.

To be a superstar can be a very different achievement to each person. Sometimes it is becoming rich and famous in Hollywood. To others it would be performing in the greatest music venues around the world. For me, I wanted to have my music performed around the world. In my idealist mind, I wanted to write the next great symphony. I wanted to change the face of the classical world. In my mind, the classical music world had stopped advancing and developing since Samuel Barber, and I was going to bring America into the 21st century. But this was hampered by my own emotional issues.

Numerous times through my music education and through my life, I would suffer through periods of depression. These periods would affect me in all aspects of my life, from my daily routine to loss of interest in television and food to not being inspired to write a single note. My professors would often notice and encourage me to try new techniques such as mapping, listening to different genres of music, or to use a notebook just to scribble down ideas for pieces. These insights would get me excited to start writing again and within the next few weeks I would create new, original music at what seemed like breakneck speeds. Many of these pieces I still adore and quite a few of them have gone on to be performed in numerous locations.

One of the aspects of being a composer that I had never thought of was the consistent devotion to at least attempting to create something. I always assumed that it would be a near constant state of inspiration and output. We are raised on these stories of Bach and Mozart using nearly every hour of their day creating new, fantastic pieces up until the day they died. They would pass on with manuscripts scattered around their deathbed and unfinished projects littering the floor or desks. Unfortunately, this isn't always true. Once my professors assured me that depression, times of inactivity, or even years of no performances was a normal situation, I felt as if things might work out or that I could possibly pursue a life in composition.

Unfortunately, it wasn't until I was in my doctoral program that I finally started to take risks and try for new adventures. In my first year studying with the late Greek-American composer, Dinos Constantinides, I sent an application into what I thought was a far-fetched goal. I soon forgot about the application and went back to studying for my exams. Near the end of the term, I received an email notifying me that I was accepted to the European American Music Alliance/Nadia Boulanger Institute. This was a far-fetched program and opportunity and I never thought I would be accepted. I quickly told my wife about the program, and we started figuring out how we were going to pay for it. After receiving grants from the university, gift money, and starting a GoFundMe, I finally had the money to fly to Paris and spend a month learning from teachers from some of the greatest music schools (Juilliard, San Francisco Conservatory, University of Pennsylvania, and the Schola Cantorum in Paris). This was a program that lit a fire under my butt and really pushed me to finish my degree. This would lead into pieces that would later be performed around the world.

Thanks to this program, I also met one of my best friends, Hillary Lester. We would later join together during the pandemic of 2020 and start a podcast we dubbed the *Sounds of the World*. This podcast is such a wonderful catharsis for the dark times of the last year. Our program was set to interview people of the musical world from around the globe. Thankfully, many of our guests have been astonishingly honest and inspirational. We have even been guests on another podcast. Our podcast has helped me with my feelings of not achieving much in my life. Their stories inspire us and urge us to keep driving forward.

I often see many colleagues going on to performances and academic positions and I quickly become jealous. Jealousy is the hardest thing for me to overcome in my adventures to achieve my dreams. The last piece to my success is the constant support from my wife. She encourages me to strive for my dreams but also reminds me of the lessons I must learn from failures or falling a little short of my desires. Much like my first composition lesson, she helps me acknowledge what I have done well, while routing me towards fixing somethings that I might need to resolve better.

While my idea of what it would be to be a superstar is different from many others, there are a few things that young people should remember before setting out to achieve their dreams. Never lose sight of what you want to achieve, be devoted to your dream, dare to take calculated risks, and always seek out the help and support of those that you admire and love. If young artists can remember these steps, I believe that they will never feel like a failure no matter how their achievement is measured.

Author Bio:

William Montgomery is an award winning and internationally performed composer based in Idaho. He also co-hosts the *Sounds of the World* Podcast with his dear friend Hillary Lester.

www.williammontgomerycomposer.com

19

A LONG, SLOW ASCENT TO SUPERSTARDOM

Christopher Norton
Canada

I started out with no expectations of being a superstar – I just wanted my work as a composer to be heard and accepted.

I arrived in the UK on a scholarship in 1977. I opted to go to York University, where the professor was esteemed writer and musicologist Wilfrid Mellers, and the music education specialist was John Paynter.

I knew I wanted to be a published composer, but I also came to the table with an unusual background – I had written orchestral pieces, a piano concerto, lots of piano music, and chamber music, but had also started to write jazz and rock pieces, influenced by four years as a high school music teacher (and by joining a band for the first time). Even before I left New Zealand, I had experimented with pieces which crossed the classical and pop divide – carefully notated music with a groove is the best way I can describe what I was trying to achieve.

John Paynter heard some of my work and recommended me to Dennis Parker, the education specialist at Universal Edition. My first UK publications resulted – all Christmas titles. One of them, *Carol Jazz*, was a book of piano improvisations on well-known carols and is still selling well over forty years later. Dennis liked my approach so much he asked me to write, in his words, "a set of graded pieces in popular styles," and I set about this with great enthusiasm. But Dennis emigrated to Canada and the manuscripts languished in the proverbial bottom drawer. It was some time later that a piano student of mine, Judi Harries, got a job as assistant to the educational music specialist at esteemed publisher Boosey & Hawkes (Rachmaninoff, Prokofiev, Shostakovitch, Bartok, Bernstein). This person was Rex Billingham, still a close friend after forty years. Rex immediately saw the potential of my "graded pieces in popular styles" and quickly dubbed the series to be Microjazz (emulating Bartok's Mikrokosmos). Then the slow climb to success began.

It was an unusual step to take for my publisher – heavily promoting a hitherto unknown composer. *Microjazz* 1 and 2 and *Microjazz Duets* 1 and 2 were the first books to appear in 1983. Inclusion of two pieces in the ABRSM syllabus helped draw attention to my range of styles, and I began to tour in the UK and Europe and as far afield as Australia to promote this brand-new series and brand-new concept. I even presented at MTNA in 1987.

Many more books followed – more Microjazz-related piano books, but also standalone books like *The Final Frontier* and *Lost in Cyberspace*, improvisations on American tunes (*Yankee*

Doodles) carols (*Swing A Carol*) and nursery rhymes (*Lavender's Kind of Blue*) and Rock and Latin Preludes. Books on improvising using Microjazz followed (*Improvise Microjazz* and *The Easiest Way to Improvise*) as well as *Microjazz* for most instruments with piano, *Concert Collections* for many instruments and more *Preludes* (Country, Eastern and Pacific).

During the forty years since I walked into Rex Billingham's office, I have written almost continuously and promoted at stores, conferences, and trade shows all around the world. Getting known as a composer can happen in a sudden, dramatic fashion, or it can happen through the sheer passage of time and the gradually spreading awareness of one's work via examination listings, inclusion in festivals and competitions, and plain old word-of-mouth.

Recent quotes from teachers:

"I think I'll go practice that "Away in a Manger" with accompaniment right now. It is gorgeous. I don't have to play "Joy to the World" because my student plays it for me every week. That one is a winner. A different one of my students plays it for every holiday recital."

"Have always appreciated your gift of music. Many of your songs and books have inspired my students to grow and continue their studies. Thank you, Christopher Norton"

"I love teaching your music to my students!"

. . .

With the advent of social media as a marketing tool, things have changed quite a lot – the composer is much more in control of what is promoted (and when). I have a Youtube channel (ChristopherMicrojazz) as well as a Facebook composer page (Christopher Norton Composer) an Instagram page and of course a website (ChristopherNorton.com.) Students and teachers can now see and hear composer (and other) performances and post their own performances for appraisal. Because of the pandemic, making personal appearances has not been an option for some time, and webinars, on-line masterclasses, and virtual conferences have become the norm.

Forty years after Microjazz pieces were first written, Boosey & Hawkes are repackaging all of my catalogue, starting with *Microjazz*, with new covers and audio links to digital platforms rather than the CDs that used to be such a feature of my publications. Even more excitingly, Boosey & Hawkes are publishing two brand-new piano books – *Microjazz Collections* 4 and 5. These contain thirty-four new pieces with great backing tracks (on all digital platforms, natch) which grade-wise sit between *Microjazz Collection* 3 and the *Preludes Collections*. The marketing of the re-package and the new books will be extensive, but still on-line rather than in-person.

I feel very satisfied that I have established a relationship with a publisher that has lasted this long (and is still a very cordial relationship, I should add). We have plans for future publications – *Microjazz Piano Duets Collection* 4 for sure, but also *Microjazz Flute Duets* with new guitar accompaniments and an entire new jazz series with accompanying improvisation-related material. There are also twenty-four Micromusicals coming out, as well as reissues (with great new audio) of the *Essential Guides to Pop Styles, Latin Styles* and *Jazz Styles*, books which first came out in 1997. There are superscore editions planned of many *Microjazz* books, as well as splendid audio recordings by UK pianist Iain Farrington (iainfarrington.com) of not only the new Microjazz piano pieces, but also of *Microjazz Collections* 1-3 and *the Microstyles Collection*.

You may get to superstar status but be open to the idea of a steady ascent.

Author Bio:
Composer and arranger Christopher Norton is universally regarded as the leader in his field. He is a New Zealand-born, now Canadian-based composer. He is known particularly for the Microjazz series and for Connections for Piano.

www.christophernorton.com

20

REACH FOR THE STARS, BUT REMEMBER WHO YOU ARE

Richard Simonelli aka JD Tucker
USA

Who hasn't dreamed of being bigger than the Beatles? Or Freddie Mercury at Wembley Stadium with 100,000 people in the palm of his hand. Or Taylor Swift singing to stadiums filled with adoring fans singing every word, of every song on her 1989 World Tour in 2015. Rock stars are the true kings and queens so it is only natural that we as musicians do everything we can to emulate them.

When we are young, we do things with "them" in mind: dress like the stars, sound like the stars, pretend you are the star. When I first started playing out with bands, I strutted around the stage like Mick Jagger and even carried around half a mic stand like Freddie Mercury. My hairstyle was Paul McCartney in the 70's, short on top, feathered long in the back. That was a really cool look. I even added an earring! I won the lead singer job in college with a band called The Cranks because of that haircut and earring. I knew most of the words but couldn't really sing that well yet. It didn't matter to the audience, who were drinking up a storm right up to closing time.

But for all the fun that I was having, something was missing. And it wasn't just the money or fame. As I was reaching for the stars, I didn't know who I was. I pretended, really well, but I wasn't Mick or Paul or Elton. Back in my room, I was a budding songwriter writing songs that were nothing like my stage persona. While I loved to be on stage, in reality, I was a lyricist first. A storyteller. And I had the gift of setting those stories to music and in doing so, I found my true musical voice. This was also therapy!

It seems like the story I always ended up telling was about me. My life. Even when I thought I was writing about someone else, these songs turned out to be what I was feeling and experiencing. They weren't just songs; they were my autobiography. They were me bearing my soul and innermost feelings. As a result, if I played these songs for others, the audience would know a lot about me. So, there I stood, frozen with self-doubt and fear any time I went to play one of my songs for anyone else. It is hard to anonymize a song written in the first person and the best ones I wrote were the ones that captured the emotion I was really feeling: love for my children, the pain of another breakup, and the happiness of knowing that love is the only way. But without a persona, how would I ever play them live on stage? I loved the audience, but how did I do my life in front of them? An insecurity paradox indeed. I learned later in life that Elton John wore all those glasses and crazy outfits because he too was incredibly insecure about his singing. The biggest selling artist and most prolific rock star in the 1970's with several number one albums and several more masterpieces was afraid while he was right in the middle of complete adoration and world domination that only a superstar could have. Yet, the onstage persona didn't cover the fear and self-doubt and the result for Elton was pain, addiction, and incredible loss of self. I find many musicians fluctuate between unabashed confidence and crippling self-doubt. Check out the Beatles "Get Back" documentary where the greatest band of all-time struggles to write songs and is fearful of playing the new songs in front of a live audience. Yet in the end. they pulled it together and wrote an album with three number one hits and several powerful songs.

As I learned to finally push through and play my songs in front of friends and family first and then to larger audiences, I found the real triumph came from the feeling I got playing one of my songs and seeing perfect strangers singing my words back to me. When it happens, it's magic. I'm not saying you shouldn't try to make millions of dollars or write a ton of hits. Go for it, we need more songs like that. Houses, cars, and swimming pools are fun, but how many rockumentaries do we have to see that end with the band crashing to the ground to realize that maybe there is so much more?

My advice? Reach for the stars, but remember who you are. And keep your feet on the ground. And always be yourself because the worst kind of lie is the kind you tell yourself. Being a rockstar or hiding behind a façade will not necessarily result in happiness or fulfillment. It can, but probably not. If you write your own songs, take the time to look inside. Find those songs that capture the essence of something you felt, something you experienced. A time, a place, a moment. Something that touches your heart and truly reaches the soul of another. These are the songs that people really want to hear. You must believe in yourself.To me, the biggest success you can have is having your song honestly connect with someone else. It may not sell the most records or even bring you fame, but I guarantee, you will be richer for it. The biggest stars will tell you their favorite song is not the big hit they have. Often, it is the song that is special to them and that also touches others.

So, reach for the stars, remember who you are, and always, be yourself.

Author Bio:

Richard Simonelli aka JD Tucker is a singer-songwriter living by the Chesapeake Bay with his two angels: his wife Angela and dog Angel. His two daughters, Adrianna and Nicole, are all grown up and wonderful!

www.jdtucker.com

21

HIGHS AND LOWS AND HIGHS

Bradley Sowash
USA

Growing up in a musical family, I decided early to be a musician. For me, the question was never what to do with my life but how to do it. In a nutshell, here's my career path (so far): local rock bands, ballet musician, society gigs, piano concerts, recordings, jazz worship leader, piano teacher, TV appearances, publications , periodicals, and pedagogue (teacher of teachers).

Along the way, I've enjoyed awards and honors, but one cannot measure oneself by the reaction of others. Bradley Sowash, a superstar? That's an overstatement. What may appear on the surface as an orderly trajectory is a much more random mix. High-profile concerts and recording sessions are high points but the day-to-day work of a full-time musician is more challenging than some might imagine. For me, a busy week could include accompanying, band rehearsals, worship leading, evening gigs, teaching, travel, and maybe a concert. A lean week meant increased marketing to keep the schedule full. When opportunities seemed elusive, my mantra was, "Work harder."

Inevitably, that led to burnout as described in this 2002 journal entry:

'I go to the gig disinterested. Just another Christmas party to play. The man in tuxedo - black and white behind a matching piano. Hired more for the look than the music. Thoughtfully positioned behind a ficus tree – indoor plant bedecked with ornaments of the season - also for looks and far from its forest roots. Setting up music equipment again. The eleventh such event this season or is it twelve? The twelve days of Christmas spent behind a piano improvising variations on standards and carols. Putting heart into it, trying to make art for indifferent listeners. About to begin. Asked to wait. A special surprise – barbershop quartet appears to sing a few seasonal favorites. Armbands and suspenders surround pot bellies – bald heads disguised beneath Santa hats. They are out of tune. Uneven time leading to mismatched phrasing. Now it's my turn as dinner is served. Continuing education from the lead singer - singing is harder than piano playing he says. No response but he continues anyway. We have to sing in tune and rehearse. All you do is push buttons. I smile. He'll get no fight from me. Hands running through the set list again, I close my eyes. Dig in on a holiday classic. Try the new rhythmic twist discovered on another gig. Explore the concept. Follow the art with or without listeners. A tap on the shoulder. Eyes open. Yes, I'll turn down a bit. Sorry. Two hours. No breaks, said the agent. A short gig he said. Back hurts anyway – built up from a busy season. Last night in a McMansion on a golf course. Arrived at the front door. You're not a guest. Use the back door - with the caterers. Fellow laborers in the hospitality industry. Watching the clock now. A gift. The VIP wants to speak so I stop 5 minutes early. A perfunctory thanks and applause for our pianist. All faces turn – some for the first time – we have a pianist? Smattering of applause. I'm introduced by the wrong name. Someone I've never heard of – wonder if he's playing somewhere tonight – perhaps under my name. Did the agent switch the contracts? I nod and pack up. Big state-of-the-art electric keyboard in a bigger case. Best there is and not even close to even a bad acoustic piano in feel or tone. It's heavy so I put it on a dolly. Amp on next followed by a crate for mics, cables, and a portable stool balanced on top. Out in the lobby now sweating under my bow tie with the struggle through the double glass doors. The hotel guy is worried about scratches. Use the loading dock next time he says. Outside, it is snowing as I lay down the dolly. Extra wheels under the handle support the front. A rope allows it to be pulled. It's red. A penguin in a tuxedo is pulling a red wagon through a snowy street. It's slippery in dress shoes. Small front wheels find a crack and the rig goes down. Lids open. A microphone rolls through the slush to the curb. One wheel is spinning. The ball bearings inside tick as they roll free from weight bearing duty. A yard sale of music equipment spread across a downtown intersection. Traffic light turns. Cars beep their horns moving in an eddy around me. Time stops. I am in a movie watching myself stare back at them – some bemused, some in a hurry, others still shopping, seeming to look for deals amidst my tools. I just stand there. It is a turning point. I know that I will never play "background music" again. Fifteen years is enough. Like talking on the phone without dialing first. Never again ask for requests. "Something by Sinatra?" I'd rather flip burgers. "Would you like a side of fries with that?" I'm done with that - a concert pianist now - transformed in one moment on a wintry street. I'm the only one who knows. It will be different – make recordings, take bows. It has to be. A pact is made – like an oath to myself: Only play when people will listen. Make every note count. Respect the music. Work it out somehow. Don't look back. Promises made and never broken. Follow the bliss, blessings will follow. Lay plans. Maybe play in churches. Offer benefit concerts to non-profits. Self-produce. Possibly teach. I leave the gig re-interested.'

Since it was clear that maintaining a singular focus on performing was making me feel stuck and unhappy, I asked myself "What else can I do with my skill set?" The answer was to reduce performing and expand my teaching. It turned out to be one of the best, most satisfying decisions I've ever made. What I didn't understand at the time was that playing countless gigs in a variety of settings and styles in order to make a living also prepared me to guide traditionally trained reading pianists into the joys of "off page" creative music making. Nor did I anticipate the opportunities and recognition it would open up including appearing on television, pioneering live online jazz piano classes, creating educational resources, presenting at conferences, and writing for publications such as this one.

So, while I'm still in the thick of it, the lessons learned so far that may help emerging musicians include:
    - Focus on goals but not so narrowly that you miss opportunities right in front of your eyes. Balance idealism with good enough. Perfection is paralyzing.
    - Be willing to be uncomfortable. In my experience, imposter syndrome feelings never go away completely. Just get on with it.

- Expect setbacks. For example, my teaching methods and books fell on deaf ears for a long time before being accepted.

Until next time, enjoy your musical journey.

Author Bio:

Bradley Sowash is a jazz pianist, composer, multi-instrumentalist, recording artist, author, and educator best known for his innovative live online group jazz piano classes, widely acclaimed keyboard improvisation books, and nine solo piano albums.

https://bradleysowash.com/

22

MY GRANDMA'S DYING WISH

Kimberley Dawn
Canada

I remember being a small girl driving down the highway in my parents' red station wagon. Making up songs and singing loudly, hanging my head outside the window. It was something about those acoustics. I would sing and make up songs the minute we hit the perimeter and all the way to Westbourne, Manitoba.

I was always told I was loud and seeking attention. I was always performing. Some called me a drama queen. I was always told I talked too much. And boy, would that ever come in handy when my career took off. Now, they pay me to talk too much.

As a small child I wanted to be either a nurse and or a rock star. I had pipes and I could sing. I always knew the music world was unkind. Some things my mother taught me was to always have Plan A and Plan B, never depend on a man, and chase your dreams but always have a backup plan.

I never did become a rock star or a nurse. But I did become a mental health care worker and an international multi award winning country music artist.

My teenage years were influenced by the great movie *Grease*, and my hero's, the legendary Ray St. Germain and Buffy St Marie. I always wanted to sing like them.

In 2000, I started dating the man who would become my husband. He was an executive at a record label and had heard me sing. I also knew him personally through family friends. It was October of 2000, my grandmother Lil Noonan was in the hospital, and I was bold to take Richard to see my grandmother. We had just started dating. It was the day that would change the rest of my life.

My grandmother was frail and looked Richard in the eyes and said, "My only wish is that the world will hear my granddaughter sing." Richard took my grandmother's words to heart and immediately booked me time in Sunshine studios. He got an engineer to record me. I picked ten songs by my favorite female singers, and we recorded my first ever demo album of tunes. We named it *Lily* after my grandmother. That launched a successful country music recording career.

That album was the first introduction to an amazing songwriter Billy Simard. While in the bread section at our local grocery mart, Richard saw an old friend Billy Simard. An amazing singer songwriter from Manigotagan, Manitoba. We were introduced and Billy was given a copy of *Lily*. He said he had some songs that would be cool for me to try and record. This was the makings of my very first large-scale album - *Kimberley Dawn I'm Going Home*.

I'm Going Home would launch me into Canadian standing. It was and is to date the biggest album. I was catapulted into stardom with the hit single *My Spirit Flies*. I completed the album of 2003 and we submitted for the Canadian Aboriginal Music Awards. I was on my first gig. I had to fly and would receive The Galaxy Rising Star. This was an award given to my superheroes in Canadian country music. This award goes to the superstars. I was receiving it on my first single ever released.

This would lead to the recording of three other albums, one of which was titled *Healing Jane*. I met Jane Chartrand, an amazing woman at the Canadian Aboriginal Music awards. She needed a voice for her album, and I was it. Jane had written a bunch of poems that would then be turned into songs. It was an album of one woman's survival and her determination to make a difference in this ever so cruel world. It was a journey through residential schools and a journey through a woman's perspective of the survival of a woman in the Kingston, Ontario women's prison as a prison guard. It was my job to give the songs a voice. It was the hardest recording project I would ever have to do.

Healing Jane garnered some amazing awards - keeper of the Spirit Award and Single of the Year at the 2004 Canadian Aboriginal Music Awards.

Built That Way was the next album recorded. It was the album I had to do on my own. Throughout my career, I had the opportunity to see the music world from both sides. The country music side and the radio side. Neither of which have been kind to female artists. And let's not get started on the fact that I am Metis. Every barrier was saying don't even do it. Don't even try.

But the voice inside of me said, "Do It."

So many people told me I couldn't. I wasn't smart enough. I didn't know the business well enough. I gathered all my pride and put together an amazing album called *Built That Way*. Legendary Chris Burke Gaffney produced the album. *Built That Way* took home rock album of the year, country album of the year, song single of the year, all that the Indigenous Music

Awards held in the United States. My music was finally being heard all over the world. My grandmother's wish was coming true.

'Til the Cowboys Come Home was my 5th recorded album, which was produced by Tom Dutiaume, my lead guitar player at the time. Tom's vocals put the album over the top and gave it a special sweet sound.

I recorded my most recent single "Wedding Day" that went around the world, written by legendary country music artist Doc Walker and produced by award winning Canadian Murray Pulver. The single was released March 27, 2020, right when the world was shutting down from the Covid pandemic. The song would not get played live for two years. It was still successful but was never really seen for the great song it is.

Why do I do it? Because of passion. I have a passion for the stage, for music, and for connecting with people.

I have determination. I have always been that girl that can't be told "you can't." I have heroes and mentors who have stood behind me to share knowledge of success and failures. But most of all, this was my grandmother's dying wish and I needed to make her proud.

Author Bio:

Kimberley Dawn is an international multi award winning Aboriginal singer and Canadian Country Music artist. She has recorded five albums to date and two singles released. With fans around the world watching her on YouTube including her album project *'Til The Cowboys Come Home*.

https://kimberleydawn.com

23

WHAT IT TAKES TO LIVE A MEANINGFUL LIFE

Christopher Siu
Canada

When I was invited to contribute a chapter to this book, I was honored. I asked myself: what makes someone a superstar? How can we define this term? I certainly don't feel like anything special, but over the past couple of years, I've started to take deliberate steps to improve my life and focus on my dream of a giving life and financial freedom.

Ever since I began teaching piano and theory as a way to support myself while in university, I always saw it as work. I was passionate about songwriting and arranging, but I never saw it as a practical path to pursue, especially with the ever-growing field becoming more competitive with each passing day. It wasn't until I discovered an online business coach and started my new Youtube channel that I realized I could monetize my passions in a meaningful way and contribute to the world while earning a living in the backend.

As I began uploading regular weekly content to my channel, I began building an audience, slowly but surely. I received wonderful feedback asking me to produce new videos on new topics, go deeper on certain subjects, and started finding inquiries regarding my services in my inbox. This affirmed to me the power of content marketing, and I knew that if I stayed on the path and continued to share what I know, it was only a matter of time until I could truly be financially free and buy back time to spend with the people I love, and do the things I've always wanted to do. In addition, I had the opportunity to work with composers and musicians I admired, simply because they heard my work and saw pieces of my content, which gave them a taste of my personality and what I could offer.

After around three years of uploading free videos, I knew it was time to launch an online course. Launching my first course was a mammoth task. It involved months of planning, recording, and editing videos, structuring it all in a cohesive format, and uploading it onto the podia platform. Upon release in June 2020, the following few months were relatively quiet in terms of sales, and it wasn't until September or October when I began receiving one or two sales a week. It wasn't much, but it proved to me that this business model really works and motivated me to continue on this path. In June 2021, I switched platforms to Kajabi (another online commerce platform better suited to my needs), and soon after, launched my membership. Fortunately, I had a successful launch, and the members have been enjoying the content and community ever since. This was another proof of concept to me because buying an online course is one thing but enrolling in a monthly subscription for a community and continued support is another. I felt more confidence knowing that I could contribute to my students' success and careers on a regular basis, and that more than anything makes it all worth it. I have three new courses launching next year, and I'm so excited to see how my business will continue to grow.

It's been roughly one and a half years since I started my online business. The model of content marketing, where you upload a piece of content (at least weekly) to grow an audience and eventually sell to them really appeals to me because it all stems from the mindset of giving first. Generosity is really what enables humankind to develop and progress, and I truly believe that if we all approach life with an abundance mindset and generosity, we will become an irresistible magnetic brand. We all have something to offer the world and sell, whether that's a product or service, so the way you present yourself in the world can make all the difference. People are tired of seeing gurus and influencers showing off their riches. People would rather follow creators who are genuine and want to give freely to their audience simply because they love what they do. You don't have to be the best, or the foremost expert in your field. Even if you're just a few steps ahead of your students, that's more than enough because you can really help them move their lives and careers forward, therefore making a positive difference to their lives.

This brings up the concept of the abundance mentality. While many people and business owners approach their lives from the perspective of not having enough, clinging on to the existing resources they possess, and fearing the competition, I prefer to approach business, and really life, from an abundance mentality. Essentially, it's the belief that there is more than enough to go around, and if we give freely, we will reap bountifully. Rather than seeing your peers as competition, view them as collaborators, so jump on calls with them, offer them your value, and you may potentially go into business together one day. Trust me, this one shift in mindset can really shape your worldly view for the better, and your business will only flourish as a result.

So, what really is a superstar? For me, being excited about my work, continuing to contribute to the world, and having the time and resources to do what I enjoy the most constitutes being a superstar. You don't have to be famous. You don't need millions of dollars. You don't even need a life of luxury. Ultimately, once you find your purpose, what makes you truly happy, and pursue that goal with determination, drive, and consistency, it will only be a matter of time until you get there. Remember to celebrate the small wins along the way. Slow and steady growth is key. You've got this!

Author Bio:

Christopher Siu is a pianist, composer, teacher, and orchestral arranger with a degree in Classical Piano Performance from the University of Toronto. He works with musicians around the world in their music with piano parts and virtual orchestration in a variety of styles.

https://www.christophersiu.com/

24

ADVENTURE IN DREAMLAND FROM EAST TO WEST

Yin Yin Huang
USA

As the Artistic Director of Acevedo Music & Arts Education Foundation, Inc, I have had the honor and pleasure of reaching thousands of music students during the past forty years and transforming many of their lives in a positive and world affirming manner through my empowerment of music teaching. I not only teach music but I also instill in them a positive mindset in creating music and through it to pursue their musical journey and achieve their goals and objectives.

Furthermore, I am also a mentor as well as a role model to guide the students to grow as a person and strive for what they are passionate for. Most of my students have pursued their musical journey and have received scholarships and have attended prestigious conservatories such as: Peabody Conservatory of Music, Manhattan School of Music, Julliard School of Music, Oberlin Conservatory, The Royal Academy School of

Music, London, England, New England Conservatory, Stanford and Berkley.

Music is the soul of every human being and has an everlasting empowerment of inner peace, tranquility, joy, and serenity. Thus, if every student is empowered to fully comprehend and utilize music within their daily lives, the potential of music achievement is unlimited. I encourage my students to bring joy to others through music and, most importantly, take active part in their communities with high moral standards and good character. Peace through music, autism awareness and unity concerts.

They also need to take an active part in serving humanity, especially during times of needs and disasters. My students over the years have taken part to serve humanity in a most dynamic manner and have raised over $56,000 for the following tragic events:

A. Indonesia Tsunami 2004 concert: to fund raise and support the victims in South Asia $ 18,000 raised.

B. Katrina Hurricane 2005 concert: to fund raise and support the victims in New Orleans, $22,000 raised to help musicians to replace their lost instruments.

C. Love Taiwan Society 2009 concert: to fund raise for Taiwan Typhoon disaster, victims in Taiwan, $10,500 raised.

D. Covid 19 relief funds, 2020 to help needy families $5,700.

One of my students, at the age of eighteen established a non-profit organization and through it, she raised sufficient funds to buy eight pianos for nursing and retirement homes in Pasadena,

Ca and San Gabriel Valley, Ca. She was recognized and honored by former First Lady Barbara Bush.

Each year, my students have taken the initiative to perform and bring needed joy and love to many people during Christmas, Halloween, Easter and in times of crisis in such places as nursing homes, retirement centers, blind centers, and senior citizens centers. They have been involved in music events dedicated to autism awareness, and unity concerts - dedicated to the Armenian Genocide, the Holocaust, and Slavery. They not only became better musicians but also made a difference around them.

It is through music that we, as a cultured and an understanding society, can survive. Music is the key to better communications and joy among our fellow human beings. Life passes like a glimpse of time. Life manifests its recourse accordingly. It endows every human with its adversities to test our strength. But, in effect there can't be a better opportune feeling than music in the lives of our fellow human beings. I had the privilege of being recognized by Congressman Adam Schiff as Alhambra Women of the Year in 2009 as well as the prestigious Model of Unity Award from Pasadena Human Relations Commission and Mayor Bogaard in 2011 in the City of Pasadena Council Chambers.

Students are our biggest assets and the future of our country, and therefore, there is no greater return on an investment than when investing in our students, especially during these difficult times that we are facing in our society with Covid -19, divisions, hate crimes, and violence. We, as music teachers and mentors must strive to encourage our students, as musicians, they have bigger and more challenging roles to play in our society than ever before. Musicians with a purpose, they can through music contribute to calmness, peace, tranquilly, unity, harmony, joy, love, and much more in our daily lives by their interactions and performances wherever they can.

Therefore, let's make our society a loving, peaceful musical serenade. After all, music is a powerful tool, so the more powerful we will become in making a better world.

"My parents always encouraged me to play for church. I love to perform for charity concerts," Huang told the Culver City News recently. "We did a Katrina Relief Fundraising in Asia for the Tsunami and a couple of concerts for the Taiwan earthquake [relief]."

I was a featured artist for the MidDay at Grace program in 2021. The concert has benefited many non-profit organizations since 2018. My benefit concert has been designated for the Grace Diner; it served more than seventy thousand meals during COVID-19. I was also awarded the Certificate of Recognition for performing at Voices in Unity Concert on September 18, 2021, from Senator Anthony Portantino, the Voices in Unity Concert, dedicated to anti-Asian hate, the Armenian Genocide, the Holocaust ,and Slavery. I am passionate and dedicated to the community and honored that the outdoor concert was well-received by 850 members in the audience.

I have truly surpassed my goal to use music as a tool of positive change in the world, as my daily piano lessons inspire others to do so as well. I will continue to dedicate my life to changing the lives of others through music and mentorship.

Author Bio:
Yin Yin Huang Artistic Director, Acevedo Music & Arts Education Foundation, Inc. She is a Classic pianist, chamber musician, piano teacher, chamber music coach, composer and multi award winning philanthropic pianist, and passionate about the international Federation for World Peace.

www.yinyinmusic.com

25

THE HEART JOURNEY TO THE STAR

Shirley Wang
Taiwan & USA

In 2012, I debuted at the Carnegie Hall as a soloist. I was standing on the Stern/Perelman Stage, with 2,790 seats spanning over five levels and acoustics that have dazzled audiences and performers for over a century. Hearing my voice coming back from the back of the auditorium after I sang a ringing high note was exhilarating. On the heel of this experience, a multi-year touring contract to take me to some of the most famous stages, including The Lincoln Center, was offered to me. It was a dream come true: I would be a full-time performing operatic soprano!

Moreover, it was particularly gratifying considering I took a break from my singing career to do the responsible thing: joining corporate America to work as a financial planner and later a human resource specialist. Walking back on stage was not a wise financial decision, but it was necessary. This contract showed me I had made the right choice.

What happened next really surprised me. After further examination, I realized what they asked me to sing did not align with my artistic vision or value. So, there were many sleepless nights pondering why I wasn't more excited or at peace. Then, finally, clarity came; I realized, "It will not change the kind of artist I am if I don't sing on these stages. But it will change how I see myself if I say yes to this contract."

So, I said no.

And now what?

A lot of time was spent taking internal inventory and wondering what all this meant. Then, finally, I decided to be my own boss, not only as a self-employed musician but also as my own artistic director. I wanted to communicate directly to the audience with a multi-sensory experience. So, I started working with several creative partners, designing concerts with untraditional programming. I tried to think from the audience's perspective. Especially those who don't usually attend classical performances. I wanted to reach new audiences and share my passion with them.

After months of hard work, we created themed concerts that included mixed-genre classical vocal literature (opera and arias), classical piano solo literature, piano four-hand works as transcriptions from orchestral work, and original four-hand compositions written for pianos, some show tunes, and jazz peppered in with multiple languages and cultures from around the world. But I wasn't done; I wanted more. So, I added visual artists on stage with me in real-time and whenever possible, bigger-than-life, movie-screen-sized original photography shown during the performances. I wanted it to be accessible; I wanted it to be impactful. And I wanted it to be collaborative.

For some reason, I never considered if it would be difficult. It was almost an obsession. I didn't know if anyone would want to book us, but by 2017/2018, we were booked for thirty plus concerts a year throughout central Florida. Some were sold-out performances. Many people would come up to me after the concerts, with tears in their eyes, to thank me for an exceptional and unforgettable experience that reminded them of beauty and humanity. We did numerous performances from 2014-2018, sharing our passion with many who had never been to a classical concert before. It was an intense and happy time for me.

Then, unwittingly, I contracted Lyme Disease from a tick bite when kayaking in 2018. I was feeling so sick all the time. Finally, during the intermission of my very last performance scheduled for 2018, I realized I had no choice but to take a break from singing. I was nearly in tears, wondering if I could get through the second half of my concert. I was in pain and thoroughly exhausted. Lyme Disease gave me terrible brain fog and a tough time coordinating my muscles. All of this was detrimental to a singer and a pianist. On top of that, I learned Lyme Disease is incurable. It was only going to get worse from that point on.

I knew pushing was futile. The only way to get through was to back off and let the flow take me and support me. Ironically, I first learned how to do this from kayaking. I dropped all my future engagements. I changed my diet, slept as much as my body asked of me, researched and learned about alternative Lyme disease treatments, and found a doctor who ultimately cured me of it. In addition, I learned to live mindfully from reading almost twenty books written by the Vietnamese monk Thích Nhât Hạnh. I am not a Buddhist, but I really appreciated the teaching. It was as if a storm had come through and made a real mess of my previously peaceful house. But somehow, I knew, after sweeping with a broom, wiping down with rags, and some straightening up, I would again have a tranquil home. Albeit it may be different with some re-arrangements. I rested in this "knowing."

Then 2020 came. It was a very intense year for those in the performing arts. We were challenged and inspired in unimaginable ways—those who were flexible and open to pivoting discovered a renaissance of creativity. It was a year when I explored a lot of newness with my imagination. I had stopped performing a year before all this hit, and 2020 gave me the permission to just be. My body had been recovering. With no future performance dates in sight, I was able to practice and learn music just for fun. As a result of my health struggles, my voice is different, my body feels foreign, and my whole person has changed. But the toughest challenge was it was impossible to make music with a pianist because of the quarantine. As a singer, my music is incomplete without my music partners.

So, I shifted my focus to a new venture, *Tuesday Conversation with Friends*, my podcast featuring performing artists from all over the world. We had stimulating conversations, and I featured exciting performances shared by these incredible colleagues. It started opening up new doors, forming new relationships, and creating new inspirations. It brings me back to my own personal music-making.

I am looking forward to my concerts in 2022 with new performance ventures in new cities, states, and continents. The music itself is magnificent. May my musical star blaze brightly in the night sky to illuminate the world with intensity and love.

This is my Why: In music, I see God. Only when I am living, breathing, and making music, I experience God fully. Music has chosen me.

Author Bio:

Shirley Wang, operatic soprano, public speaker, podcast host, and international bestselling author. She has performed across the U.S., including the Carnegie Hall. Podcast: *Tuesday Conversation with Friends* features those who make the world more colorful.

https://linktr.ee/ShirleyWang

26

NOTES FROM MISS MAC

Tim Topham
Australia

Thinking back, what got me started in the music business was the love of my teacher and the enjoyment I had of childhood music lessons. I had absolutely no intention of being a music teacher and probably thought, with childhood arrogance, that it would be a daggy and crazy profession to be in, but I absolutely loved my teacher. She was happy to help me in every way especially with the music I wanted to learn.

And she made lessons fun. I still keep up with her today despite the fact she has had a stroke and is in a home and is no longer able to be the musical person she was. But there are still glimmers of her old personality and she still loves hearing my stories. I became a music teacher because I wanted to pass on the love of music Miss Mac gave to me.

When I started to teach music I realized, despite my degree and teaching diploma, I had no idea what I was doing! I returned to Miss Mac (this was before her stroke) and she took me under her wing. She had just retired and so it was like a new lease of life for her. It was a formative time for me, and I learned so much from her. This was when I realized Miss Mac had revolutionized my life. She encouraged me to watch videos and attend conferences, soaking up as much information as possible about the musical world.

But what I learned was that most students don't get the experience that I had. It was awful to think that so many students were being forced into this very limited perspective of what music education is. You're going to learn three pieces a year, you're going to be examined on that, and then you're going on to the next three pieces for the next year's exams. That was the music system in Australia and much of the UK for decades. I was shocked to realize this because I knew that so much of the experience I had had in music came from the creative "out of the box" teaching that I had received.

And my music experience had gone in so many different directions as well. After I'd completed most of my study with Miss Mac, I said, "I don't like this classical music anymore."

I got to grade six, which was a good level. I was twelve at the time. I asked if I could move on to jazz and she said, "Yes." She taught me some jazz music but then sent me to Steve Sedergreen, one of Australia's most famous jazz pianists, and I studied with him for three years. After that, I moved into playing in bands, followed by musical theatre, and then orchestras at school. This led to musical direction and musical theatre production as things blossomed.

I found I had the ability to conduct bands and orchestras and even play multiple musical instruments (even if badly).

It was Miss Mac who gave me the confidence to follow my dreams and step out to do all of this, including being in a band. She made me realize I didn't have to be stuck in a classical music box or stay as a pianist – I could be a drummer or a percussionist and spread my musical wings. In turn, I wanted to give this gift to my own students, the gift of growing as a musician and trying many different musical challenges, confidently and enthusiastically, knowing they could be whoever they wanted to be.

I may be giving you the impression that my life and the musical journey were easy, but it did bring its own challenges. The past two years during the Covid pandemic have been difficult. Trying to run a small business from home whilst everyone in the family is at home is not easy.

Productivity levels dropped significantly, which I found difficult as I am a naturally driven person. The sudden lack of control frustrated me as did the fact I had to change the way I did everything and conducted my business. Also, changing people's views about music education can take time, and this can be challenging. So, I decided to start creating courses as a way to pass on my passion to others, and my membership grew from this. It took five years of grit and determination, but I then realized I had a business. Throughout this, I remembered the passion and freedom that Miss Mac gave to me. I encouraged my students to learn the type of music they wanted to learn in the first instance. I taught them pieces they could play for family and friends and which would inspire them to play. I wanted them to develop a mindset that they were blessed to have the teacher they did. Through this, you are allowing them to grow.

However, it was when I realized other teachers were following me that I knew I had a legacy to pass on. That blew my mind, the fact others were emulating something I had started, or indeed that Miss Mac had started all those years previously. That was the genesis of our TopMusicPro Community - providing a place where I could mentor all the teachers around the world who weren't lucky enough to have their own Miss Mac.

My business grew organically, and I now have a team of people who help me. This means I am able to help so many others and I am grateful for this. However, I now develop business plans and run it as a professional company, something which I should have done from the start. This does not mean I am no longer passionate, as I am, it means that this passion is on a sound business footing and will hopefully live on beyond just me. And now that we're an established and respected enterprise, I am so much more able to help future generations find their own musical passion.

I would still call myself a vulnerable leader, but I am a leader whose mission in life is to support the music teachers of the world ,and this all came about because of Miss Mac being willing to allow me to step out and grow as a musician. For this, I am forever indebted to Miss Mac.

Author Bio:

Tim Topham is on a mission to inspire and empower instrumental music teachers to create motivating lessons to maximize student engagement through creativity, technology, and innovation whilst providing the training and resources they need to run streamlined studio businesses.

https://topmusic.co/

27

A MUSICAL JOURNEY FROM JAPAN TO BERKLEE

Yoshie Nakayama
Japan

I grew up with a mother who was the music director and organist of our church. She was also a music teacher at home. I loved lessons with her. In middle school, I started to play euphonium. I also loved singing in the choir.

When I was at Kunitachi College of Music in Tokyo, I encountered big band jazz while studying music education. I really wanted to join them, but I was already a member of a student brass band and euphonium is not part of a big band so I started playing the trombone.

My joy in singing also remained active with a student choir that won a national competition. I enjoyed singing acappella songs by TAKE 6, The Real Group, VOX ONE with friends as well.

I graduated with the Japanese Music Instructors License for middle and high school but ended up taking an office job. By having a stable job, I could enjoy trombone with big bands and singing in acappella groups.

After ten years, I realized I had spent time and money for Kunitachi and was not using the education. At the same time, the skills I had didn't match with what I was into. I enjoyed more contemporary music and jazz but the education I had at Kunitachi was based on classical music.

I wrote to a Berklee professor, the founder of VOX ONE, Yumiko Matsuoka, and asked her opinion. She recommended that I join a summer camp that she was instructing.

It was a week of summer camp for choral singing in Connecticut hosted by a vocal sextet, Western Wind. My intention was to see how much I'm compatible with talented singers since my interest in my career change was something to do with acappella.

The camp was something I had never experienced before. The group I got in were all professionals. The speed of improving new songs every day was amazing. On top of that, I was surrounded by passionate people who dedicated their week to singing all day. They ranged from high schoolers to elderly people which would never happen in Japan.

When the camp was over, Yumiko suggested that I should go to Berklee if I'm still not sure what to do next. Also, the fact that my skills didn't match with what I wanted to do supported the idea. Then I came to realize I want to produce acappella music. Going back to school was never in my wildest dream but studying and living abroad was something I always wanted.

A few weeks later, I applied to Berklee.

I had so much to learn for the audition. Within the following few months, I joined a music school in Tokyo that uses the Berklee method. The teacher gave me the basic knowledge so I could start off somewhere in the middle of the program. He also advised me to declare trombone as my principal instrument since they needed trombone players which are less popular than vocalists.

By the end of the year, I also started taking trombone lessons from another Berklee alumni and prepared for the audition which was in mid-February.

My audition was successful. I was accepted to Berklee with a scholarship.

Studying at Berklee is a life-changing experience. Before coming to Boston, my Japanese friends asked me why I would go so far away and spend money never mind the language barrier. I didn't have the answer back then but after I came here, I understood why. There are legendary, EGOT award-winning teachers and many amazing opportunities I would not otherwise have had.

While I was excited to be there, the language barrier got in my way. I remember my first week, a teacher asked the class, "Who reads notation every day?" I did not understand what notation meant. So, I started to make non-Japanese friends.

I graduated from Berklee with a major in Contemporary Writing and Production. Now I could write, record, and produce not only acappella but also any style.

During the three years at Berklee, I had great experiences. One of the biggest moments was to be a music producer of Multi-Latin Grammy and Grammy winner Alejandro Sanz's performance on a live broadcasted show by Univision, the biggest Latin TV broadcasting company in North America. The event had an audience of 8000.

In 2017, I moved to LA and started teaching piano while freelancing with skills that I could offer. In July 2021, I received a message from one of my Berklee teachers that there would be an opening to teach at Berklee. I was so excited. As much as I liked living in LA, the opportunity to be able to teach at Berklee was beyond anything else. I applied right away. Followed by a

Zoom interview that included a demo class to the Department Chair and the Assistant Chair, I got the job offer on August 6, and moved to Boston on August 31.

Although I was used to teaching piano, teaching in a classroom was completely new to me. Some students could not understand what I was teaching no matter how well I prepared, especially international students just like me during my first semester. I have been dedicating my time to helping these students understand better.

International students must overcome so much to follow their dreams. Many of them face bigger issues than the average student. I find them inspiring as they deal with the challenges to learn music to achieve their career goals.

I am now proud to be an Assistant Professor at Berklee. I teach arranging courses including Vocal Writing, which is arranging for the band with vocalists and acappella. This is the course that led me to apply to Berklee to learn to produce acappella music. Teaching the exact course is a full-circle moment for me.

When I think about my life, I feel so fortunate to be in my current position since I am now able to help teach the musical superstars of the future. Music is the language that took me from Japan to Berklee. Where will the language of music take you?

Author Bio:

Yoshie Nakayama is a Music Producer, Arranger, Trombone player, and Singer. A Co-Founder of Songs for World Peace as well as Assistant Professor at Berklee College of Music. Yoshie's arrangements are available at Sheet Music Plus.

https://www.yoshie-music.com

28

AFTER A LIFETIME

Ray St. Germain
Canada

The climb to Superstar can take a viral instant in today's world of modern media technology.

But in my early beginnings as a singer, songwriter, recording artist, and award-winning television host, my climb was more about climbing into the backseat of a station wagon, driving all night to the gig, performing, then packing up and doing it all over again the next day. In fact, my good buddy, the late Dave Dudley sang his hit song "6 Days on The Road" on my television show called *Ray St. Germain Country*. As I look back at my over fifty years in show business… I've sung just about everything.

My first television appearance was on a cross-Canada singing competition called *Talent Caravan* on CBC-TV in 1958. It was the *Canadian Idol* (*The Voice*) in its day. The winner was decided by mailing in votes from across Canada. Although I was making a living on the road performing as Winnipeg's

Elvis with the *Hal Lone Pine Show* (US recording star) and his son jazz legend Lenny Breau, opening for Grand Ole Opry stars such as Johnny Cash, George Jones, Johnny Horton, Porter Wagner, etc., I decided to enter the contest. The show was live from the Playhouse Theatre in Winnipeg. I sang a Billy Grammar song called "Gotta Travel On". I was the only country singer on the show. I didn't think I had a chance. There was a jazz singer, an opera singer, and many others. Much to my surprise, I won. That was the beginning of my television career. In 1963, I was called by producer Ray McConnell at CBC-TV to audition for a new Big Band show called *Like Young*. I got the gig and sang Big Band songs and hosted the show that ran for thirteen weeks. Between TV shows, it was back on the road for performances.

This led to me becoming the singing host from Winnipeg on a new national TV series called *Music Hop Hootenanny* 1964 - 1966, on the CBC network – thirty-nine shows a year. Alex Trebeck hosted from Toronto, (and went on to host *Jeopardy*). We sang rock and roll, folk songs, and even a little country.

I went on to guest host on other TV specials such as *Show of the Week* and *In Person*. My guests included Ian and Sylvia Tyson, Gordon Lightfoot, Anne Murray, and a host of stars in Canada.

Flying back and forth to Toronto to host CBC Specials and guest on the *Tommy Hunter Show*, I had a chance to reunite with Anne Murray. She made a guest appearance on *In Person* from Toronto and we had a great time singing a duet together. At that time, I was co-hosting with Pat Harvey an hour TV special for CBC called *Two for the Road*. Anne Murray was one of our guest performers as she had just recorded her first album and was on her way to becoming a Superstar, with her song "Snowbird".

I went back to Toronto for a new variety CBC television show called *Time for Livin'*, and I became the singing host. This time it would be a big band show with the Rick Wilkins Orchestra featuring members of the award-winning *Boss Brass*.

They had me sing everything from country to big band swing... an incredible experience.

It seemed as when one show was canceled, another TV opportunity would open up. An entertainer's life is full of ups and downs. The climb to the top is sometimes difficult, with many obstacles to overcome along the way, but the view from the top is magnificent.

My next adventure led me to the CBC television show called *My King of Country* and featured Nashville stars taped in front of a live audience. It was the first CBC show from Winnipeg to feature Nashville recording stars such as Lefty Frizzell, Carl Smith, Dave Dudley, Bobby Bare, Tom T. Hall, and more.

The final frontier.

After years of travel and moving, there was one more television show series that would be closest to my heart. Why? Because it became a family affair.

In 1978, I was delighted to produce, write, and become the singing host of our award-winning television show called *Ray St. Germain Country*, which later became *Big Sky Country*. It received the Gold Medal for Outstanding New Variety Program at the Can/Pro Awards. This was a proud moment to celebrate.This national TV series ran for thirty years until 1990. The proudest moment of these years was that all five of my children performed on the *Big Sky Country Show*: my daughters Chrystal and Cathy (who co-hosted *Ray St. Germain Country*), sons Ray Jr. and David (DJ), and youngest daughter Sherry and my grandson Jeff. My wife Glory was my "behind the scenes" support person, who has been on this musical ride with me for over forty-five years.As my television shows came to a close, the radio world opened up. In 1998, I joined the Manitoba Metis Federation to learn more about the organization and my Metis people. I was then invited to produce a radio show called *The Metis Hour*. The show airs on the NCI radio network and is heard worldwide at NCIfm.com. I owe a huge debt of gratitude to the Manitoba Metis Federation and President David Chartrand for starting me on my radio broadcasting career.The show expanded to two hours and became *The Metis Hour X 2* featuring Manitoba Metis Federation President David Chartrand giving weekly news updates, along with music featuring Metis Artists, and my co-host Naomi Clarke and I taking live calls for guests to celebrate and say hello. I am also grateful to NCI-FM Manager Dave McLeod for his continued support.

I am grateful to have made my passion for singing, performing, and producing into a profession that I continue to cherish to this day. I am also grateful to have received numerous awards including the Aboriginal Order of Canada, Country Music Hall of Fame Inductee, MACA Entertainer of the Year, Song of the Year, Recording Artist, Best Country Album, the Golden Award - Recognition for Lifetime Achievement, Order of Manitoba and many more.After a lifetime of singing, entertaining, producing, and hosting television and radio shows, playing stages big and small, big band to solo acts, being a travelin' man performing in various venues and across countries, my music legacy lives on through my many recorded albums. My favorite song, that I've ever written is "If You See the Same Bird, You'll Know That It's Me". Why? Give it a listen... *may it inspire your why.*

Author Bio:

Ray St. Germain is a singer/songwriter, recording artist, television host & producer. He has received the Lifetime Achievement Award, Order of Manitoba, Queen Elizabeth II Diamond Jubilee, Aboriginal Order of Canada and is in the Canadian Country Music Hall of Fame.

https://www.facebook.com/ray.s.germain

29

THE CLIMB TO REACH THE STARS

Glory St. Germain
Canada

As I look back at my life's journey, I can still vividly see the image of myself as a young girl, alone in my bedroom - admiring the posters of superstar musicians hanging on the wall. I would pretend that I was a superstar too. Yes, I was singing into the mirror, *hairbrush microphone* in hand, never before seen dance moves, playing my imaginary keyboard while blasting Beatles music from my record player.

I was living the dream of a superstar in the making. Little did I know, the beginning of the climb over many obstacles to reach the stars had just begun. The stage was calling me. I always aspired to be on the big stage as a keyboard player and singer in a band. My grandpa used to say, "If you wish upon a star, and you believe with all your heart, your dreams will come true."

Isn't it funny, that when you are a kid, you believe that you can do anything? My grandpa even told me so. Yet, later in life, as you think that you have become wiser, why is it that you start to doubt yourself? An opportunity to audition for a superstar band looking for a female keyboard player was posted in our local newspaper. At the age of seventeen, I was not only excited beyond my wildest dreams about the audition, but I wanted this more than anything. It was my ticket to the stars.

By now, I had become a piano teacher, running my own successful music studio and still only performing in front of the mirror for my imaginary fans. So how hard could performing on stage possibly be? After all, my years of *hairbrush microphone* training should count for something, right? As I stood at the back of the concert hall, music bag in hand, it seemed like a defining moment for me. Everything I wished for, the stage, the lights, the music that I loved, it was all there waiting for me. I watched the other girls audition for the band as I sat silently, going unnoticed at the back of the room. They were all so incredible, so beautiful, so talented. I was in awe of these musicians. This little star of mine was not shining brightly that night. I felt that I was not good enough, not talented enough, and I simply walked out the back door without ever doing the audition. I was so disappointed in myself, the opportunity of a lifetime, my dream of becoming a star, had just passed me by.

Was it really a failure or simply a pivot to an opportunity that was yet to come? I realized that my dream was to create something different. To help students and teachers around the world to shine brightly in their own learning as I created the Ultimate Music Theory Workbook Program, writing over fifty books with my writing partner Shelagh McKibbon-U'Ren and creating the UMT Teachers Membership with my Creative Design Manager Joanne Barker.

Years later, I realized that this life lesson experience had taught me that I needed to climb, one star at a time, and to never give up the superstar dream. I remember getting on stage and presenting a music teacher's workshop in front of hundreds of educators. This time, there was no walking out the back door. This time, I embraced the opportunity to speak into that *hairbrush microphone* and impact the audience with my revolutionary talk to embark on a life-changing direction for me as a global music educator.

Listening to the needs of fellow educators led me to create the Ultimate Music Theory Certification Course for Teachers. Why? Because I knew I could help teachers overcome the obstacles faster if I simply gave them the tools to do so quickly, so they didn't have to go through years of searching for answers as I did.

In life, we have a choice - to dream big and reach for the stars or to accept failure and never grow to our full potential. Perhaps the stage as a musician was not where my star was shining the brightest, perhaps it was shining inside of me as a speaker.

The star that shines brightest on the stage for me is my husband, Ray. His "marshmallow voice" still melts my heart, as do the voices of our children and grandchildren - all singers.

In 2021, I created the Global Music Teachers Summits and hosted expert speakers from around the world to connect thousands of music educators at a deeper level - with topics of discussion that are sometimes left unanswered, but necessary to help us grow through professional development.

This led to a global community of musicians - all of whom have become international best-selling authors as I published five books in *The Power of Why Musicians Series*. This anthology book series with 125 musicians/authors from around the world will impact its readers for years to come with their stories of inspiration, as they too have overcome obstacles in their lives and risen to success.

The realization came to me. We not only pivot in our lives, but also evolve.

I had developed my music business skills gradually, from a single star to a more complex form of educator, course creator, and international best-selling author.

Why wish upon a star? Because my grandpa said, "If you believe with all your heart, your dreams will come true." A lifetime dream of mine was to become a TEDx Speaker.

I wanted to share my knowledge and ideas worth spreading to educate the global music community. My wish upon a star was a dream come true, not only once but twice.

From the little *hairbrush microphone* to the global speaking stage, I was honored to present two TEDx Talks in 2021. (Yes, you can watch them on YouTube… *no hairbrush microphone seen*).

Today, as an Ultimate Music Teachers Business Coach, I continue to wish upon a star, not for me, but for you. I want to serve you at the highest level. Help you reach for the stars and achieve your dreams because dreams do come true - if you believe with all your heart.

If you wish to learn more about the Ultimate Music Theory Certification Elite Educator Program and are interested in working with me, simply go to UltimateMusicTheory.com to contact us. Discover your Why. Together, we can make your star shine bright like a diamond in the sky.

Author Bio:

Glory St. Germain ARCT RMT MYCC UMTC, Founder/CEO Ultimate Music Theory, TEDx Speaker, International Bestselling Author in The Power of Why Musicians Series, 50+ Ultimate Music Theory Books, and Course Creator of the UMTC Elite Educator Program.

https://UltimateMusicTheory.com/

ABOUT THE AUTHOR

Glory St. Germain ARCT RMT MYCC UMTC Founder/CEO, TEDx Speaker, International Bestselling Author 50+ Ultimate Music Theory Books & The Power of WHY Musicians Series. Host of Global Music Teachers Summits, Expert Coach & Creator UMTC Elite Educator Program.

Glory is the Founder/Author of fifty books in the Ultimate Music Theory Program and Founder of the Magic of Music Movement. She is on a mission to help one million teachers create a legacy through their businesses. She is the host of the Global Music Teachers Summits, Course Creator, Expert Music Teachers Coach, Publisher of the Ultimate Music Theory Series, and an International Bestselling Author in The Power of Why Musicians Series, an anthology of global authors/musicians sharing their stories of inspiration.

She is the founder of the UMTC ELITE EDUCATOR PROGRAM - A Business Accelerator in knowledge and expert strategies for teachers to use in order to run their successful music studios. She empowers educators to elevate their income, impact their teaching, and build their expert music business while enjoying personal time for self-care, family, and pursuing other passions.

In addition, Glory is an NLP Practitioner (Neuro-Linguistic Programming) and has taught Piano, Theory, and Music for

Young Children for over twenty years and contributed as a composer. She has served in various leadership positions to support music education organizations.

Glory has spoken on many international stages presenting workshops and is passionate about enriching lives through music education.

Glory loves learning and especially loves books on business and psychology. Mindset is a subject she believes has the potential to change our outcomes. Mindset is limited only by our own thinking. She is a Positive Mental Attitude Advocate and strongly believes that we need to see mindset as a priority, not only for ourselves but also for how we help others think, learn and grow.

She is married to Ray St. Germain, a professional multi-award-winning entertainer and Canadian Country Music Hall of Fame inductee. They have five musically talented children, many grandchildren, and the family continues to grow.

Glory lives her life with gratitude, passion, and serving others through her work.

https://UltimateMusicTheory.com

ACKNOWLEDGMENTS

I want to thank all the musicians for being willing to share their stories of inspiration and most importantly their WHY.

Their WHY became the driving force that compelled them to stay the course, to never give up, and ultimately led them to climb to superstar in their industry. I am grateful to them and proud to share the power of why their dreams became a reality in this book.

I want to thank my "UMT Dream Team" Shelagh McKibbon-U'Ren, Joanne Barker, and Julie-Kristin Hardt who helped me to implement these ideas and share them with the world.

Thank you to the hundreds of musicians, entrepreneurs, teachers, and students that I have learned from through the years who gave me the framework to build my company, write the Ultimate Music Theory Program, UMT Courses, UMT Membership, and compile the *Power of Why Musicians Book Series*.

Special thanks to our editors Wendy H. Jones and Lisa McGrath for their guidance, expertise, and countless hours in making this book possible.

It is with gratitude to everyone who has taken the risk to dream big and follow their heart to become a musician, composer, educator, or entrepreneur, and generously leave their legacy by enriching lives through music education.

Special Thanks to the Why 29 Musicians Climbed to Superstar Authors:

Randall Faber, Rami Bar-Niv, Matt Becks, Dorothy Chia, Louise Earhart, Cebo Carr, Joanne Barker, Paul Myatt and Gillian Erskine, Cate Friesen, Ray St. Germain Jr., Doreen Hall, Karen Hedges, Shumaila Hemani, David A. Jones, Dominique Levack, Rebecca Featherstone, Ivy Leung, William Montgomery, Christopher Norton, Richard Simonelli (JD Tucker), Bradley Sowash, Kimberley Dawn, Christopher Siu, Yin Yin Huang, Shirley Wang, Tim Topham, Yoshie Nakayama, Ray St. Germain Sr., and Glory St. Germain.

AFTERWORD – THE MAGIC OF WISHING ON A STAR

Glory St. Germain

Have you ever wished upon a star? It seems like magic, doesn't it?

Why? Because when you believe in the magic of wishing upon a star, you may get your wish. However, wishing comes with a desire, dedication, and determination to achieve a goal.

As I reflect on the powerful stories in all five books of *The Power of Why Musicians Series*, I see a common thread among them… and that is, the power to dream, to reach for the stars above all setbacks or obstacles to overcome.

I am proud of each and every one of the musician/author-contributors who are kind enough to share their story of WHY they do what they do. Their stories are here to inspire you to take a leap of faith and live your truth.

To wish is to feel or express a strong desire or hope for something that is not easily attainable. When you wish, you have a true sense of yearning.

As a musician, author, and friend, my wish for you, is that

AFTERWORD – THE MAGIC OF WISHING ON A STAR

you reach for the stars. Go for it! What will it feel like, look like, and sound like when you reach your star?

I have experienced many ups and downs in my life, as many of us have. But my greatest joy has come from wishing, dreaming, and making things happen.

May you be inspired to wish upon a star... play your music proudly, teach the world to sing, share your passion and make *this place* a better place.

If you wish upon a star and believe with all your heart... *wishes really do come true.*

There is magic in wishing on a star.

Many Blessings to you and may your life shine brightly.

ALSO BY GLORY ST. GERMAIN

The Power of Why 21 Musicians Created A Program
The Power of Why 23 Musicians Crafted A Course
The Power of Why 25 Musicians Composed A Legacy
The Power of Why 27 Musicians Captured The Lead

www.ingramcontent.com/pod-product-compliance
Lightning Source LLC
Chambersburg PA
CBHW072021110526
44592CB00012B/1397